Ng'ambo Atlas

Historic Urban Landscape of Zanzibar Town's 'Other Side'

Department of Urban and Rural Planning, Zanzibar

African Architecture Matters

Table of Contents

List of Maps

Historical Maps and Plans

Survey Maps

Foreword

Certain periods in the course of progress determine history. The years 2011-2015 have been a decisive moment in the modern history of the urbanisation and urban development of Zanzibar. In 2011, His Excellency the President of Zanzibar, Dr Ali Mohammed Shein, decided to create a fully-fledged Department of Urban and Rural Planning (DoURP) in Zanzibar. In 2012, DoURP started a review of the National Land Use Plan of 1995, in order to draft a new Spatial Framework for the Islands: the National Spatial Development Strategy (NSDS), adopted in 2015. During 2011-2015, DoURP took daring decisions to craft an innovative vision of urban development, and an inspiring philosophy of urbanisation, to influence sustainable development.

Although the New Urban Agenda (NUA) was already underway, DoURP started to advocate for inclusiveness, liveability and sustainability. Since the adoption of the UNESCO Recommendation on the Historic Urban Landscape (HUL) in 2011, the department has endeavoured to link HUL and NAU. Hence, under the NSDS, urbanisation is encouraged to harvest its positive transformative power to the full, and, at the same time, culture is strongly promoted so as to foster identity of national community and spirit of place. As such, NSDS targets liveable and compact cities and towns, while making culture a driver and an enabler of sustainable development.

One of the NSDS goals is the development of two cities and 14 local towns in the Islands. In order to achieve the urban development objectives, the Zanzibar City Master Plan proposes a New City Centre, in the *Ng'ambo Tuitakayo: Zanzibar Town City Centre Local Area Plan* (also known as the Ng'ambo Local Area Plan). The planning of the New City Centre is a testimony of the link between NUA and HUL. The new Ng'ambo Local Area Plan crystallises the idea of an inclusive and liveable city by promoting mixed use, prioritising walking in safe streets, and developing public open space, but it also encourages reasonable density to enhance social and economic dynamism. It is important to emphasise that one of the four pillars of NSDS is the environment.

Since 2000, the Stone Town of Zanzibar has been inscribed in the UNESCO World Heritage List, and part of the Ng'ambo area is a buffer zone of the World Heritage Site. Yet, with the HUL approach, Ng'ambo has stopped being merely a protective layer of Stone Town and becomes an enhancement layer for the social and economic dynamism of the City Centre. By doing so, the buffer zone is not only safeguarding the heritage but also promoting culture, protecting urban values and enhancing the socioeconomic dynamism of the City Centre by linking the 'old town' and the 'inner city'.

This significant change to the planning process has been achieved thanks to important preparatory work realised in adopting the HUL approach. The exhaustive field work was carried out between 2015 and 2017. With a team of motivated architects, students and volunteers, a full inventory of the Ng'ambo area was made. The *Ng'ambo Atlas* is a result of that groundwork, demonstrating the transformation process of the old spatial framework of the Swahili world towards its modernity. Understanding and recognition of the cultural significance of an urban setting to facilitate management of change is an important toolkit in the HUL approach. As happened in Stone Town nearly 150 years ago, Ng'ambo is now taking a new course in history. I believe that the result of this extensive work merits documentation and presentation, so that local and international communities may better appreciate Swahili culture and civilization in depth.

I would like to take this opportunity to thank my colleagues at the Department (today under the Commission for Lands) for supporting me, and for their dedication during the preparation of the Ng'ambo Local Area Plan. I wish to convey my gratitude to the Government of the Netherlands, especially the Dutch Embassy in Tanzania, and to the City of Amsterdam for their generous support to the Government of Zanzibar in realising the Ng'ambo Local Area Plan, which is part of this work. I would also like to thank Stadsherstel Amsterdam for their support throughout the process. My sincere thanks to AAmatters for their enthusiasm in preparing the Ng'ambo Local Area Plan and the *Ng'ambo Atlas*.

Muhammad Juma,
Director (DoURP)
Zanzibar

Introduction

This atlas is the concluding chapter of the Ng'ambo Tuitakayo project undertaken by the Department of Urban and Rural Planning in Zanzibar and African Architecture Matters, in collaboration with the City of Amsterdam between 2012 and 2016.

The goal of the project was to prepare a local area plan (structure plan) for the new city centre of Zanzibar's capital. From the beginning, our planning exercises were grounded in the notions of urban culture and heritage, while the principles outlined in the UNESCO Recommendation on Historic Urban Landscape provided us with a framework for the subsequent stages of our work. It did not take much time before we realized that the cultural and historic richness of Stone Town's 'Other Side' merited a wider recognition than a technical planning document would allow for. For this reason we decided to collect our findings in this atlas - a format that on the one hand enabled us to bring together and present Ng'ambo's rich planning history through historic maps and plans, while on the other to draw attention to the outcomes of the mapping of the material and immaterial cultural landscape conducted during the project.

It is not that the urban history of Zanzibar Town has not been studied before. However, a comprehensive publication attempting to bring together material and immaterial, past and present aspects of Ng'ambo's urban culture, has, to our knowledge, not yet seen the light. The research and work of William Cunningham-Bissell, Laura Fair, Garth Andrew Myers, Abdul Sheriff and others have proved to be of great value to us and are aptly used as references throughout the publication. Still, if we compare the amount of available academic and popular literature on Ng'ambo to that existing on Stone Town, it is not difficult to see that the 'Other Side' of Zanzibar Town has, over the years, been granted considerably less (inter)national attention.

As with many other African cities, Zanzibar Town has been subjected to spatial and social colonial planning, resulting in an arbitrary division of the city along racial lines. In this process Stone Town was designated as the 'European, Arab and Asian Quarters', with Ng'ambo as the 'Native Quarters'. The 1964 Zanzibar Revolution eradicated the racial lines dividing its capital city but was unable to unmake the division between an elitist and a popular half of the city. Local and international perceptions of the cultural and historical importance of its respective neighbourhoods have thus for a long time remained overshadowed by the social and cultural divisions created during colonial times. Needless to say, the complex colonial and post-independence development of the city has shaped its contemporary environment, and is evident in its urban tissue and cultural activities (or lack of such in some cases) across the area.

One thing which is certain is that despite the limited international fame and recognition of its importance, Ng'ambo has played and continues to play a vital role in shaping the urban environment of Zanzibar's capital city. It is difficult, if not impossible, to compress the diversity, dynamic and complexity of the place onto the pages of an atlas. We realize that the selection of subjects included in this publication is incomplete and there are both gaps and limits in the material presented on the following pages. However, we consider this atlas above all as a reference work, and hope that it can be an inspiration and invitation for readers to deepen and broaden the research into the cultural riches of Ng'ambo, which, together with Stone Town, form the beating heart of Zanzibar.

The major organising principles of this publication are time and materiality; the latter understood as the architecture of the area and the intangible cultural practices that take place within it. In the first chapter of the atlas we provide a broad outline of the history of Zanzibar Town in general, and Ng'ambo in particular. Through maps, surveys, plans and images we recount the story of the city and its people and create a background to the following chapter. While the first chapter is a purely historical account, the information presented in the second chapter is a combination of oral histories, field surveys and historical research. In Cultural Landscape of Ng'ambo the reader may explore through maps and accompanying texts and images the architecture of Ng'ambo, as well as subjects such as toponymy, cultural activities, public recreation, places for social interaction, handcrafts and urban heritage. In the third chapter, Swahili Urbanism: Conclusions and Reflections, we bring together our observations, findings and conclusions regarding Ng'ambo. In the two final chapters we describe the history, context and methodology of the Ng'ambo Tuitakayo project.

We trust readers will find this book a helpful initial portal into the cultural and historical riches of Zanzibar Town's 'Other Side'.

Zanzibar – Amsterdam, 2018

The Editors

Team and Contributions

This publication is based on research and material produced during the preparation of the Local Area Plan for Zanzibar Town City Centre (Ng'ambo Area). The LAP was a joint initiative of the Department of Urban and Rural Planning in Zanzibar, the City of Amsterdam, and African Architecture Matters. The plan for the Zanzibar Town City Centre was approved by the Revolutionary Government of Zanzibar on 13 May 2017.

The work of the team was coordinated by the director of the Department of Urban and Rural Planning in Zanzibar, Muhammad Juma and Antoni Folkers from African Architecture Matters. The following individuals were core-team members of the planning team: (DoURP) Muchi Juma Ameir, Mohammed Badruddin Mussa, Abdallah Rashid, Rabia Hamisi Selemani. (AAM) Amélie Chauvin, Berend van der Lans, Marie Morel, Alexandra Papadaki and Iga Perzyna.

The survey team, in addition to the full-time planning members, was composed of the following members: Belinda van Buiten, Cisem Caglayan, Mia Callenberg, Johanna Ericson, Marloes Hamelink, Maike Lühr, Marieke Oosterom, Lucas Luis Oteyza, Rebecka Peterson, and Maria Sjöström.

A number of professionals were involved on a part-time basis and contributed to specific aspects of the work including Amina Issa Ameir, deputy principal secretary at the Ministry of Information, Tourism and Antiquities; Issa S. Makarani, director-general at Stone Town Conservation and Development Authority, and Nicole Bolomey, who served as a heritage expert and adviser to DoURP. In addition, the following people were involved with the project steering committee: Ruwan Aluvihare, senior designer at the Department of Planning, City of Amsterdam; Sabine Gimbrère, director at the International Office, City of Amsterdam; Mzee Khamis Juma from Zanzibar Municipal Council; Berend van der Lans from African Architecture Matters; Paul Morel, senior project manager at Stadsherstel Amsterdam; Mwalim A. Mwalim, chair of the Zanzibar Road Fund, Aart Oxenaar, director of the Department of Monuments and Archaeology, City of Amsterdam; Keimpe Reitsma, senior consultant, City of Amsterdam. The following individuals contributed to the publication: Mwalim A. Mwalim kindly gave his permission to re-print an excerpt from his unpublished book in the *Ng'ambo Atlas*, while Salim Said Salim shared a short story on the loss of trees in Zanzibar and place naming.

Acknowledgments

Many government officials, organisations, professionals and individuals provided support and advice and participated directly in the preparation of the Local Area Plan for Zanzibar Town City Centre (Ng'ambo Area). The planning team would like to acknowledge the guidance and assistance provided by the offices of the Government of Zanzibar during the project period. In particular, the team extends its thanks to Mr Abdi Mahmoud Mzee, former urban district commissioner; Mr Abdallah Mwinyi Khamis, former regional commissioner; directors in the Land Commission, Said S. Ufuzo, Mwalim M. Hamad, and Mwanamka M. Abdulrahman (previously in Land Commission); Dr Amina Issa Ameir, deputy principal secretary at the Ministry of Information, Tourism and Antiquities; Issa S. Makarani, director-general at Stone Town Conservation and Development Authority.

The team would also like to thank each and every Sheha of Ng'ambo for facilitating research and contact with informants in the areas under their jurisdiction, providing the team with invaluable information and guidance.

A number of organisations and bilateral donors helped and contributed to the process: we extend sincere thanks to the Netherlands Enterprise Agency, which supported the research that was executed in the context of the collaborative project between Zanzibar and Amsterdam which forms the basis of this publication, and the Embassy of the Kingdom of the Netherlands, the City of Amsterdam and Creative Industries Fund for funding the preparation and printing of the *Ng'ambo Atlas*.

We would also like to thank the Dutch Minister of Trade and Development, Mrs Lilianne Ploumen for touring with us through Stone Town and Ng'ambo, which kick-started the project. In addition, we would like to thank the Dutch Ambassador Jaap Frederiks for his interest and support, as well as embassy staff and in particular Monique Korzelius, Renet van der Waals, Hinke Nauta, Lianne Houben, Neema Matafu and Eugene Gies for their support and advice. We also thank Rosalind Boschloo from the Netherlands Enterprise Agency (part of the Ministry of Economic Affairs) for her assistance in setting up the project.

The team would also like to thank all the people who contributed their time and knowledge to this publication for their reviews of the manuscript and precious comments. We extend our special thanks to the numerous informants who contributed to our understanding of Zanzibar Town, and who have provided the information that forms the basis for this publication.

We would also like to give our special thanks to Farouk Topan and Prof. Abdul Sheriff, who reviewed the chapters on the historical development of Ng'ambo and cultural landscape and added several important changes. Prof. Sheriff, in addition, also served as an advisor on the history of Zanzibar Town throughout the project. A similar thanks goes to Mwalim A. Mwalim who assisted us throughout the process with his incomparable knowledge of the heritage and culture in Zanzibar.

Finally, our wholehearted appreciation goes to the inhabitants of Ng'ambo, without whom this project would not make sense.

1

An Historical Outline of Ng'ambo, the 'Other Side' of Zanzibar Town

Zanzibar Town is the capital city of the Zanzibar Archipelago. The city is located on the western coast of Unguja Island, the main island of the archipelago, which lies in the Indian Ocean, off the coast of East Africa. Several names are used interchangeably in literature on Zanzibar when referring to its capital city and the areas within it. In addition, the name of Stone Town is often mistakenly taken for the name of the entire city, of which it is only a part. To avoid confusion with regard to use of names, in this publication they are applied in the following way:

'Zanzibar Town' is understood as the entire capital city. However, the focus of this publication will be on the areas which form the core of the city. Ng'ambo (sometimes also referred to as the historic Ng'ambo), is understood as the area located between Benjamin Mkapa Road (also known as Creek Road) to the west and Felix Moumie Road to the east. Stone Town is the part of the city located on the tip of the peninsula and stretching to the Creek Road in the east.

According to the 2012 census, the population of Ng'ambo numbered around 32,000 inhabitants. However, this number may be considerably higher, as indicated by figures collected during the Ng'ambo Tuitakayo research in 2016, which revealed some 57,000 inhabitants.

Fig 1.1: Map indicating location of Zanzibar Town on Unguja Island

I. Ng'ambo Tuitakayo Base Map (2015)

Ng'ambo Tuitakayo Base Map indicating borders of the area depicted in this atlas.

Topography

Zanzibar Stone Town was built on an old coral reef. The other half of historical Zanzibar Town, Ng'ambo, was built on the land side of the intervening creek. The creek itself was gradually reclaimed during the first half of the 20th century, leaving only Funguni Basin to the north as a body of open water. The reclaimed creek, now recognizable in the alignment of Mkapa Road, is the natural geomorphological western boundary of the area. The geomorphological boundaries to the north and south consist of the coast. The eastern boundary is a natural depression between the second and third old coral reef ridge, running in a north-south direction, defining the geological configuration of the western tip of the island. The main bulk of Ng'ambo's building stock is built on the slopes and the ridge of the second old coral reef. The highest elevation point is in Michenzani area. The lower-lying areas at the perimeters are generally less densely developed, which can be explained by the fact that they are prone to flooding.

II. Geomorphic Map of Zanzibar Town (1927)

A contour map based on the 1927 survey of Zanzibar Town (see map VII).

Ng'ambo: the 'Other Side' of Zanzibar Town

The historical Ng'ambo of Zanzibar originated as a suburb of Zanzibar Town. Meaning, literally, the 'Other Side', Ng'ambo is a common way of referring to 'the other side of a place' in Kiswahili (the term is also used to indicate the 'overseas'). In the case of Zanzibar, Ng'ambo was not only a geographical reference to the area starting to develop across the tidal creek separating the peninsula from the main island in the mid-19th century, but also a metaphoric one. Over the years, the two parts of town developed a mutual relationship touching on all levels of sociocultural, economic and urban aspects of life. While the nature of this relationship may have changed over time, the two parts of town nevertheless maintained an ongoing connection, which was manifested in various ways during particular periods in history.

The story of Ng'ambo is woven from many varied threads and cannot be properly understood without looking at the broader context of Zanzibar Town. The diverse origins of its inhabitants, varied provenance of the merchants passing through the city in the old days, tourists visiting today, and the foreign background of some of the rulers of Zanzibar over the past two centuries, have all left their mark on its urban landscape. The cosmopolitan nature of the city was further enhanced in the material realm by the work of, among others, the British, Chinese, East German, Indian, Israeli, Norwegian and Tanzanian planners and architects who, over the past century, were together responsible for the city's rich history of urban planning.

Zanzibar Town can be read as a palimpsest of the multiple layers of culture brought in by different social groups over the years, yet in essence it has remained a Swahili city. It developed over time from a few *diko* (tiny temporary fishing settlements) into a typical East African island merchant town. After becoming the new seat of the Omani rulers in the late 18th century, it was only a matter of time before Zanzibar Town claimed the position of the uncontested capital of the Swahili world from Kilwa, Lamu and Mombasa, around the 1820s. There was no other city in East Africa that could compete with Zanzibar Town during the 19th century, neither in number of inhabitants nor in strategic military and economic importance. Zanzibar Town lost its leading position only after the emergence and growth of the new colonial capitals of East Africa at the turn of 20th century.

Through all the turmoil and change, despite prolonged periods of foreign dominance and notwithstanding rigorous modernist rebuilding plans under the socialist government of the late president Karume, the city retained its distinctive Swahili urban character. Its Swahili character was (and is) manifested through Swahili houses built around mosques, merchants' palaces, markets and *barazas*, and in a bustling creativity and collective outdoor life. Dance, music, sports and other cultural expressions have been an inherent part of the day-to-day life of people in Ng'ambo, shaping their local identity and communal feeling.

By the 1930s, the structure and size of Ng'ambo was approximately the same as it is today. What is more, a closer comparison of historical maps from the turn of the century and the 1960s with current maps, reveals that many of the names existing in the past survive today. Place naming is discussed in more detail in the following chapter. However, it is worth mentioning that while the names as such might have remained in use, their geographical reference has changed over years, confirming the fluid nature of the city. The cultural research conducted during this project has also revealed that many of the historical, sociocultural and economic characteristics of the area persist up to the present, manifested in its multi-layered urban environment.

From *Diko* to Island Metropolis (up to 1891)

The origins of Zanzibar's capital city can be found at Shangani, once a strategic location for a *diko*. Until the end of the 16th century, the settlement was of no political, cultural or economic importance, while Unguja Ukuu, the former capital of the Unguja Island, and Makutani on the neighbouring Tumbatu Island, were thriving cities. By the end of the 16th century the island was ruled by a local dynasty under Portuguese control. Until recently, the only known vestiges of the Portuguese presence in the area of Zanzibar Town were that of a chapel and adjoining merchants' houses, but new excavations have uncovered other remnants from that time.[1]

The Portuguese were ousted from Zanzibar by the Omanis in the course of the 17th century. Structures that were left behind are said to have been incorporated into the fortifications built by the Omani rulers before 1710, the same ones which were later transformed into what is today known as the 'Old Fort'. In the 1820s, Seyyid Said, the Sultan of Oman, decided to transfer his seat of power from Muscat to Zanzibar, which boosted the growth of the city. As capital of the Omani empire, Zanzibar became, in the 19th century, what Major F. B. Pearce called the Island Metropolis of Eastern Africa, as a consequence making Zanzibar Town the most important city in the area.

Fig 1.2: View of Forodhani after the English bombardment in 1895

Fig 1.3: Contemporary view of Forodhani and the House of Wonders
Forodhani has been the heart of Stone Town since the mid-19th century, when it served as the main customs area in town. The port buildings were later transferred to reclaimed land in Malindi, while the warehouses located in Forodhani were removed in 1928 to create a large open space in front of the palace complex. Parts of the open space were rehabilitated in the early 2000s as a public park. Forodhani continues to be one of the major gathering points for the residents and tourists alike, with its famous night market serving food and beverages.

[1] For more information on recent excavations in Stone Town see http://www.archaeology.org/news/5806-170811-zanzibar-colonial-excavation.

Fig 1.4: Contemporary view of Forodhani

Expansion of Zanzibar Town to the 'other side' commenced not later than the 1840s and most likely much earlier than that. As indicated on Guillain's map, the size of Ng'ambo was already substantial by 1846. The suburb grew at a rapid pace, and by the end of the 19th century its size exceeded the original settlement on the peninsula. The development of Ng'ambo was concentrated along the road to Mtoni (*chemin de M'tony*), the only passable overland road of importance at the time, leading to the main palace of Sultan Seyyid Said. The bridge between Stone Town and Ng'ambo was located where Darajani Street today meets Creek Road (*Darajani* means 'at the bridge'). The second bridgehead shown on Guillain's map was located at the current junction of Malindi and Mkapa roads.

From early on, the population of Ng'ambo consisted of many different ethnic and social groups. It was home to merchants, freed urban and plantation slaves, fishermen, traders, boat-hands and labourers from the islands of the Indian Ocean and mainland, as well as migrants from the *shambas* in Unguja. The number of nationalities living in Ng'ambo at the turn of the 19th century is revealing, and includes populations from various parts of Asia, from Hadhramaut, Comoros, Madagascar, Somalia, Ethiopia and East African lands corresponding to today's Malawi, Mozambique, Congo and mainland Tanzania.[2] The various social and ethnic groups inhabiting Ng'ambo transplanted their own cultural forms into the city through crafts, music, dance, names and customs, traces of which can still be found in the area.

The immense wealth of the commercial empire that Zanzibar became by the mid-19th century was concentrated in few hands, something which was also reflected in the local landownership. Most of the land on which Ng'ambo was developing belonged to landowners from Stone Town. The majority of landowners considered the lands in Ng'ambo as their *kiunga*, meaning properties closest to town.[3] Apart from being a description of landownership, the term *kiungani* can also be understood as a description of the ideology of interdependence that linked the rich and the poor in the area, through the give-and-take relationship between patron and client.[4] Over the years, large parts of the land owned by magnates from Stone Town were bequeathed to their former slaves under *wakf*, as rent-free plots for the poor and destitute.[5] The *wakf* lands were administered from the mosque by the *mutawalla*, or the *wakf* administrator.

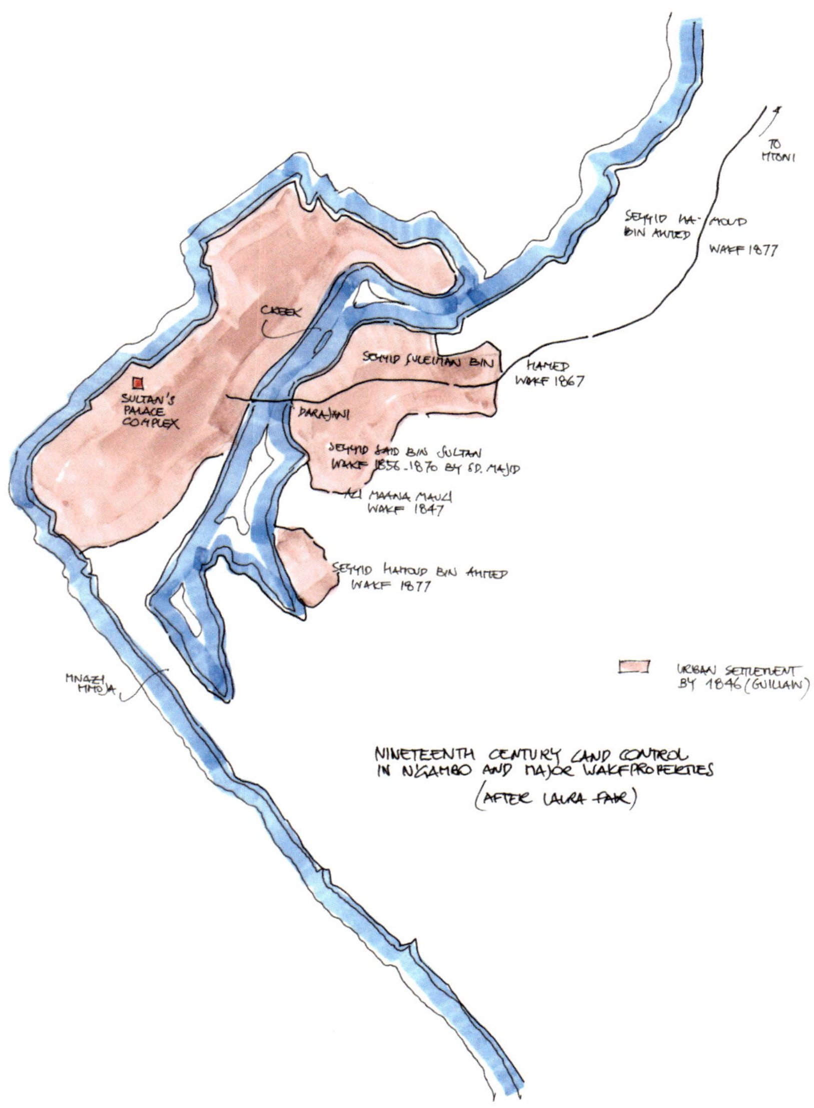

Fig 1.5: Nineteenth century land control and major *wakf* properties, drawing after Laura Fair

2 Garth Andrew Myers, "The Early History of the 'Other Side' of Zanzibar Town", in *The History and Conservation of Zanzibar Stone Town*, ed. Abdul Sheriff (Ohio, Ohio University Press, 1995), p. 39.

3 Ibid., p. 36. To read more about the use of term *kiungani*, see also: Laura Fair, *Pastimes and Politics: Culture, Community and Identity in Post-Abolition Urban Zanzibar, 1890-1945* (Ohio, Ohio University Press, 2001), pp. 113-129.

4 Myers, p. 114.

5 *Wakf* is a 'permanent dedication of property for a religious, pious or charitable purpose' under Islamic law, with no intention of reclaiming it.

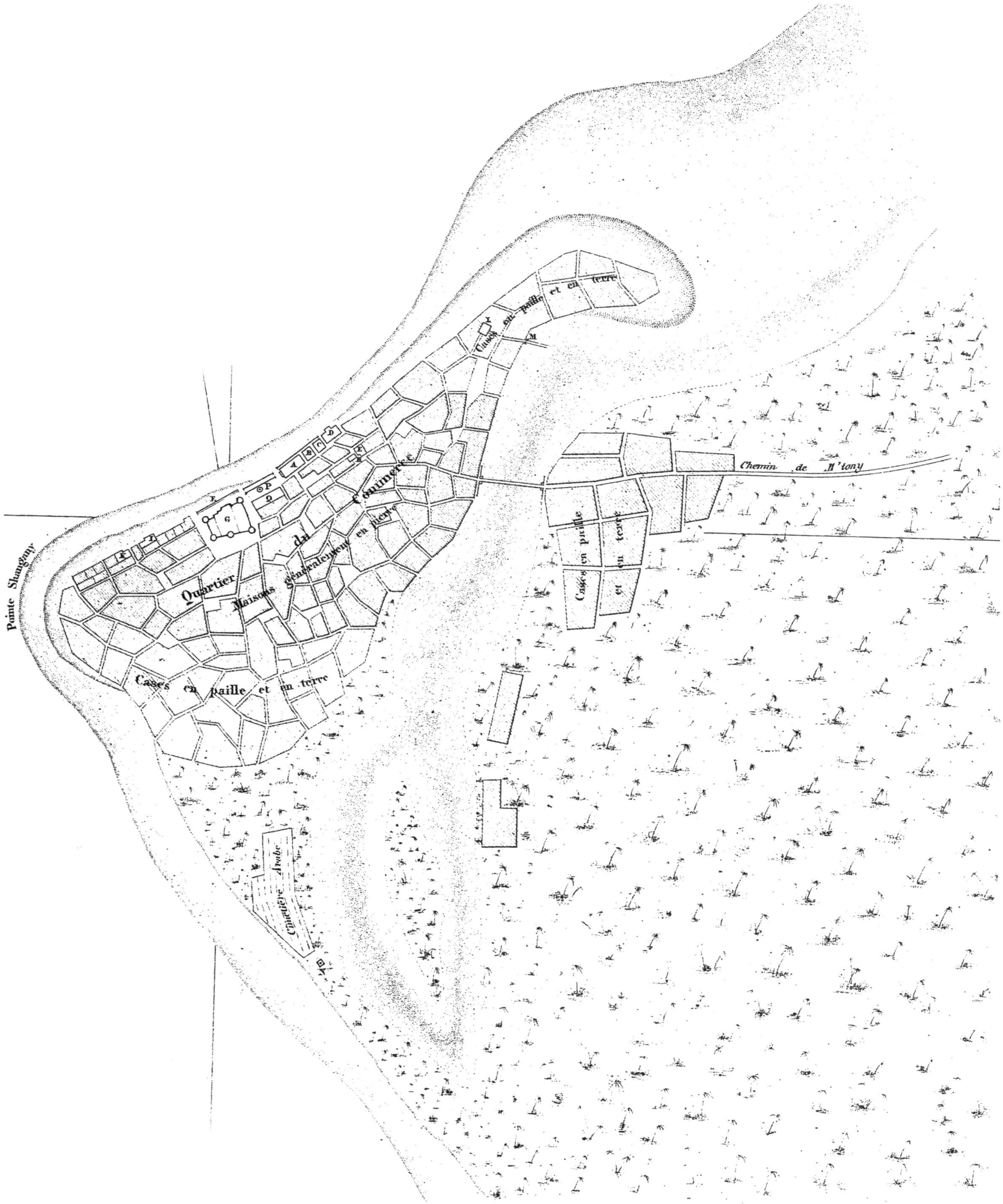

III. Map of Zanzibar Town by Captain Guillain (1846)

Captain Guillain's travelogue is one of the most detailed and lavishly illustrated works on East Africa from the mid-19th century. The distinction between stone houses (maisons généralement en pierre) *and mud huts* (cases en paille et en terre)*, employed later on by the colonial government to justify the segregation of the city following the line of the creek, can already be seen in the map.*

From early on, Ng'ambo was divided into a number of small neighbourhoods known as *mitaa* (sing. *mtaa*). Each *mtaa* varies in size and character. The extent of one *mtaa* is not always clearly defined by urban edges, making it at times hard to distinguish their exact borders on the map. As in Stone Town, most of the wards in Ng'ambo have their own mosques, which in many ways serve as the social and religious centre of the neighbourhood. By 1895 the area already comprised 15 *mitaa*, whereas in 1910 when the area was divided into Police Precincts, 26 residential *mitaa* were mapped around their respective mosques. Despite substantial administrative changes over the years, a comparison of the contemporary survey with the survey from 1927 shows that the number of mosques in the area has not diminished, but grown by two, confirming the continuous importance of these religious institutions in the organisation of the neighbourhoods (for further information on the role of mosques in the organization of *mtaa* (*see* Chapter 2, pp. 97 and 136).[6]

From the mid-18th century until the imposition of spatial and racial urban division by the colonial authority in the 1920s, the urban tissue of Ng'ambo did not differ much from that of Stone Town. Both sides consisted of stone-built houses and houses made from mud. The basic grain of the urban tissue, as was the case in many parts of the historic Stone Town, was (and remains today) the Swahili house: a free-standing single-storied rectangular building with a little walled-in courtyard at the rear and outhouses for services. The arrangement of the Swahili houses within the neighbourhoods followed an organic pattern. The historic tissue that had developed by the 1920s continues to be visible in the contemporary urban tissue of Ng'ambo.

Fig 1.6: Swahili house
Example of a typical single-storey Swahili house.

Fig 1.7: Mantondoni village on Lamu Island
Example of typical Swahili urban tissue.

Zanzibar Town, types of houses, 1893

Source: Survey of Zanzibar Town, 1893, National Archives Zanzibar. Redrawn from *The History and Conservation of Zanzibar Stone Town*, ed. Abdul Sheriff (Ohio, Ohio University Press, 1995).

[6] For more information on importance and history of mosques, see "Mosques, Merchants & Landowners in Zanzibar Stone Town" in *The History and Conservation of Zanzibar Stone Town*, ed. Abdul Sheriff (Ohio, Ohio University Press, 1995).

By the advent of British colonial rule, Ng'ambo had grown to a similar size as Stone Town. Jointly, the two parts formed a truly cosmopolitan city with various communities with Arab, Swahili, Indian, Persian, Comorian, Goan and Madagascan people, to name a few, living next to each other in wattle-and-daub Swahili houses, Omani *beyts* and Indian *dukas* on both sides of the creek. By the end of the 19th century, Ng'ambo consisted of a dense amalgam of stone houses concentrated in the areas around Darajani, the Swahili urban tissue, agricultural land, recreational grounds, graveyards and suburban villa estates. Together they formed a green and pleasant suburb on which foreign visitors not infrequently commented more positively than on the overcrowded Stone Town.

"*The cleanliness of the roads, lofty groups of palm and mango trees scattered between the huts, and the cheerfulness of the population, composed of all Central African tribes, makes Ng'ambo the most attractive part of the city.*"[7]

Fig 1.8: Street in Ng'ambo in the late nineteenth century

Fig 1.9: Earliest known photograph of Ng'ambo
Picture taken from Malindi looking southwest.

[7] "Die Reinlichkeit der Strassen, die reizenden Gruppen von Palmen und Mangobäumen, die zwischen den Hütten verstreut sind, und die Munterkeit der aus allen Stämmen Centralafrikas zusammengewürfelten Bevölkerung machen das Ngambo zu dem anziehendsten Teil der Stadt", in Oscar Baumann, *Der Sansibar-Archipel. Ergenbnisse einer mit Unterstützung des Vereins für Erdkunde zu Leipzig 1895/96 ausgeführten Forschungsreise. Zweites Heft. Die Insel Sansibar und ihre kleineren Nachbarinseln* (Leipzig, Duncker & Humblot, 1896), p. 31.

The main growth vector of Ng'ambo, as in Guillain's times, continued to be in its northern part along the Mtoni road, now forking into roads towards the rural towns of Mkokotoni and Chwaka. Other new roads connecting Stone Town with Ng'ambo starting to emerge at the turn of the 19th century are the southern road, and the path crossing the tidal creek following the natural depression at Kisiwandui. It is important to note the presence of recreational facilities at this early date: a tennis court, a club, a canteen and a number of pleasure gardens, of which the gardens in Mwembeladu, near the fork in the Mtoni road, are the most conspicuous. Another large villa with gardens was built around this time by Mselem bin Mohamed Al-Khalasi, a wealthy landlord who was also employed as a colonial official.

The open grounds surrounding the built-up areas of Ng'ambo most likely already served the inhabitants of Zanzibar Town for recreation before the installation of the British Protectorate. A closer look at the development of the area from 1892 until the present day reveals that the main open grounds have been in continuous use for sports and recreation ever since. The activities taking place on the grounds might have changed from the exclusive elitist games of golf, tennis, hockey and polo to football or netball, but their primary use has been retained. As indicated by Laura Fair, recreation and sports have played a key role across the years in shaping the relations between the residents of Zanzibar Town.[8] Findings of Ng'ambo Tuitakayo have confirmed the continuing importance of sports in moulding the local identity and strengthening community pride among the residents of town.

Fig 1.10: Mselem House

The house of the rich businessman and landowner Mselem bin Mohamed Al-Khalasi, located in Kikwajuni. Mselem was known for taking advantage of his position to exploit the poor. He was sentenced to hard labour in the town quarry, not for stealing from the poor, but for embezzlement of government funds.[9]

Fig 1.11: Tennis court at Mnazi Mmoja

In his account of Zanzibar published in 1919, Major F. B. Pearce described Mnazi Mmoja as one of the most attractive recreation grounds in Africa with one of the prettiest and greenest golf links, football grounds, cricket pitches, croquet lawns, and several excellent tennis courts under the management of the European Sport Club.

Fig 1.12: Football players at Mnazi Mmoja

[8] For more information on the impact of sports and recreation on shaping relations between the inhabitants of Zanzibar Town, see Laura Fair, *Pastimes and Politics: Culture, Community and Identity in Post-Abolition Urban Zanzibar, 1890-1945* (Ohio, Ohio University Press, 2001).

[9] Laura Fair, "Voice, Authority, and Memory: The Kiswahili Recordings of Siti binti Saadi", in *African Words, African Voices: Critical Practices in Oral History*, ed. Luis White, Stephan F. Miescher and David William Cohen (Bloomington, Indiana University Press, 2001), pp. 246-263.

IV. Map of Zanzibar Town by Imam Sharif (1892)

The map was drawn by Imam Sharif, a land surveyor of Indian origin. It is the first survey of Zanzibar Town recording all the built structures in the city. The survey enabled the newly installed colonial administration to gain better knowledge of the city, and served the tax system they introduced to the island well. It is the first record of Zanzibar Town after the 1846 map and shows the substantial growth the city had experienced over a period of only 50 years. By 1892, the core of Ng'ambo as we know it today was already in place.

British Colonial Dream Town (1891-1963)

It could be argued that the British were not the first colonial power in Zanzibar, but were preceded by other powers including Persians in the distant past, the Portuguese and the Omani. From the period when the islands of Unguja and Pemba were under the rule of the Sultan (who at the time also controlled larger parts of East Africa) until the installation of the British Protectorate in Zanzibar in 1892, there was a famous saying indicating the strategic importance of the archipelago: "*When the flute plays in Zanzibar, they dance on the lakes*".

This situation underwent a drastic change after the division of East Africa into colonies among the European imperial powers, with their respective capitals in Nairobi, Kampala and Dar es Salaam. Even though Zanzibar Town remained the largest city of East Africa by the turn of the 19th century, with more than 60,000 inhabitants in 1895, its strategic importance in the 20th century went into decline. By comparison, the region's second largest city, Mombasa numbered around 30,000 inhabitants in 1906. Nairobi was just established, and in 1906 numbered only 11,500 inhabitants, while the number of inhabitants in Dar es Salaam reached, at most, 20,000 souls around the same time. By the 1930s, Nairobi had outgrown Zanzibar Town, soon to be followed by Dar es Salaam and Kampala.[10]

The declining strategical importance of Zanzibar may be one of the explanations for the fact that the British administration on the island was rather thin and fragmented throughout the more than 70 years of colonial rule. Only a restricted number of colonial officers was available to govern the islands; from a handful during the early years, to just over a hundred in the seemingly well-organised administration in the later years. But as organised as this administration seemed on the surface, it was permanently unable to meet its goals due to understaffing and weak officers.[11]

[10] Population in major African cities at the turn of the 20th century. Figures derived from Colin Rosser, *Urbanization in Tropical Africa: a Demographic Introduction* (An International Urbanization Survey Report to the Ford Foundation, 1972): Abidjan 1910 - 1,000, Accra 1901 - 26,622, Addis Ababa 1908 - 35,000, Dakar 1904 - 18,400, Dar es Salaam 1900 - 20,000, Ibadan 1890 - 200,000, Kinshasa 1908 - 4,700, Lagos 1901 - 41,000, Mombasa 1906 - 30,000, Nairobi 1906 - 11,500. For statistics on population growth in Zanzibar between 1835 and 2002, see table in Antoni Folkers, *Modern Architecture in Africa* (Amsterdam, SUN Architecture, 2010), p. 73.

[11] To read more about urban planning during the British Protectorate and challenges faced by the colonial administration's bureaucratic system, see William Cunningham Bissell, *Urban Design, Chaos and Colonial Power in Zanzibar* (Indiana, University Press, 2012); Sarah Longair, *Cracks in the Dome: Fractured Histories of Empire in the Zanzibar Museum, 1897-1964* (London, Routledge, 2015).

V. Map of Zanzibar Town by Oscar Baumann (1895)

Oscar Baumann was an Austrian consul in Zanzibar at the end of the 19th century. The map he drew for the report on his travels around East Africa comes very close to what can be considered as a tourist map. The 1892 survey served as a base map on which Baumann highlighted places of interest, including palaces, gardens, consulates and the post office, as well as places of cultural or natural interest such as Mwembe Ngoma *or* Tanzplatz *(the dance place at the Mango tree) or* Shimo la Tarya *(the cave where the drum was kept).*

Colonial Stage Set

"Zanzibar might have been one of the most beautiful cities in the world. Built as it is on a spit of land jutting out into an azure sea, studded with green islets, and backed by verdant hills covered with waving palms, it should have no rival. Nature has done her best, but man has failed to take advantage of his opportunities. Even as it is, Zanzibar seen from the sea is attractive in appearance, but one looks in vain for the pinnacle mosques and the glistening domes of an Eastern city."[12]

One of the central personalities in the early years of the British colonial rule was John Houston Sinclair, who arrived on the island around 1895. Sinclair was trained as an architect, but decided instead to pursue the career of a colonial officer, and would eventually make it to the position of Resident in the 1920s: the highest ranking British official on Zanzibar. Besides his administrative role, Sinclair designed a large number of buildings that were erected in the early years of the British Protectorate, such as the Central Court, the Post Office and the Residency. He was an avid enthusiast of Saracenic architecture and introduced its features into many of the buildings he designed.

The Omani architecture dominating the skyline of Stone Town is sparse in decoration. This may be explained by the fact that the Omani were followers of the Ibadi sect of Islam, whose architecture is geometric and plain, and avoids ostentatious and decorative elements on the exterior of buildings, as does traditional Swahili architecture. The orientalist champion and traveller Richard F. Burton remarked as early as 1872 that the skyline of Stone Town evoked a 'puritanical plainness'.[13] The austerity of the island's architecture was regarded by colonial visitors as a shortcoming, which from the aesthetic point of view caused damage to Zanzibar.[14] Hence, it became one of the ambitions of the early colonialists to remodel the city in a manner that would suit its oriental setting.

In his attempt to alter the skyline of Zanzibar, Sinclair set out to create a colonial stage set that would conform to the ideas about the Orient broadly held by Europeans. His endeavours served in many ways to create a true heterotopia: the making of an orientalist town silhouette befitting the perceived image of Zanzibar - an Arabic city with sultans, princesses, palm trees, minarets, pointed arches and cupolas. At the time of Sinclair's arrival on the island, Zanzibar was indeed ruled by a sultan, there were princesses - like the famous Seyyida Salme - and palm trees in abundance, but no minarets, pointed arches and cupolas conforming to the orientalist perceptions of the East.

In 1923, the architect and urban planner Henry Vaughan Lanchester made a visit to Zanzibar to draft a masterplan for the future development of the city. It is no coincidence that Lanchester's proposal for the redevelopment of Zanzibar's waterfront coincided with Sinclair's Residency and met the Saracenic, or Sinclairist aesthetic expectations. Apart from the proposed redevelopment of the seafront, Lanchester also planned the location for Sinclair's Peace Memorial Museum which was to be the pinnacle of the transformation of the plain skyline of Zanzibar into a Saracenic townscape. Sinclair's ambitions were never fulfilled, but through his public buildings Saracenic features were introduced to the landscape of Stone Town, and his influence continued to be felt in buildings constructed as late as 1950s.

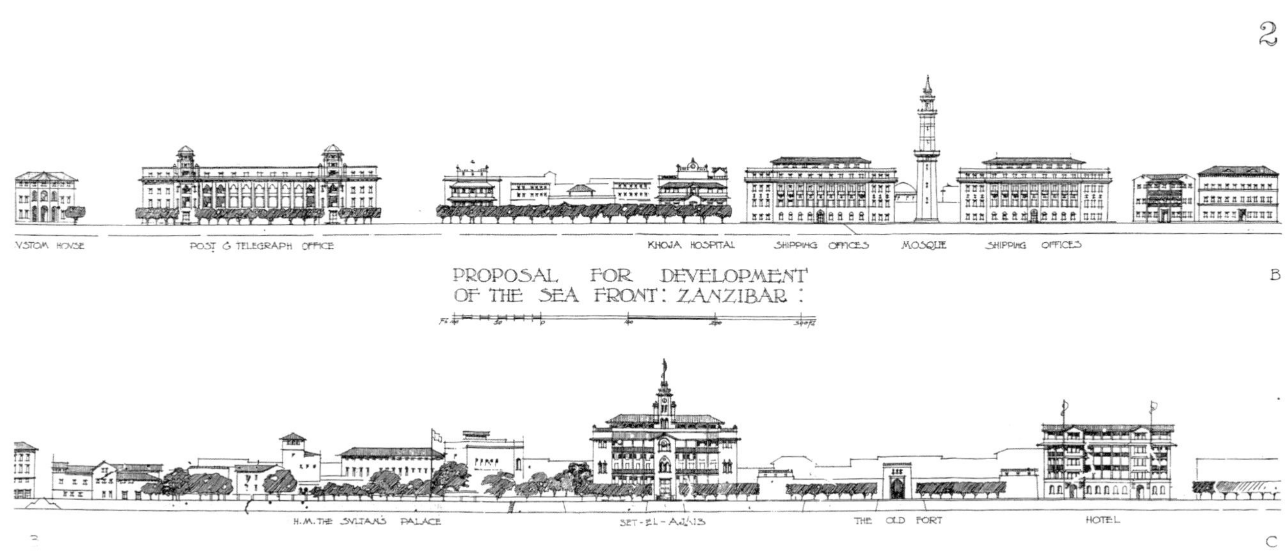

Fig 1.13: Design for Stone Town waterfront by H.V. Lanchester

Lanchester admired the location and potential of the city, but had little appreciation for how it presented itself to the sea. His masterplan included a rebuilding of Stone Town's waterfront in a monumental manner, with elements of the Saracenic style planned for buildings used for administrative and commercial purposes.

[12] H. V. Lanchester, *Zanzibar: A Study in Tropical Town Planning* (Cheltenham, Burrow, 1923), p. 29.

[13] Richard Francis Burton, *Zanzibar: City, Island and Coast* (London, Tinsley, 1872), p. 32.

[14] F. B. Pearce, *Zanzibar: The Island Metropolis of East Africa* (London, T. F. Unwin, 1920), p. 146.

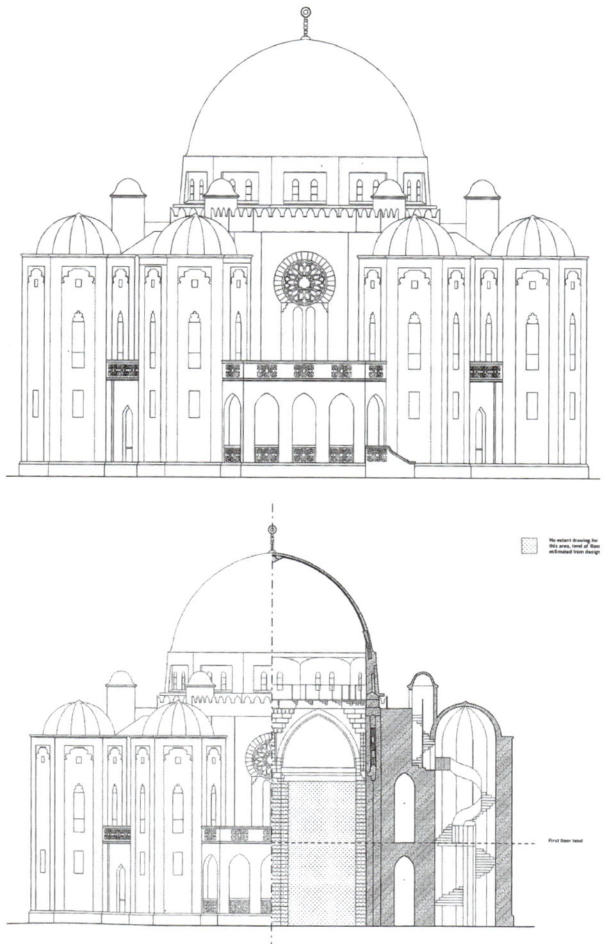

Figure 2.11 Reconstruction of 1920 design, using 1920 façade and dome from 1923 design. Drawing by Livia Wang.

Fig 1.14: Peace Memorial Museum: reconstruction of the 1920s design, drawing by Livia Wang

The Peace Memorial Museum, located on the border of Stone Town and next to the Mnazi Mmoja grounds, was the crowning project of Sinclair's dream to reshape Stone Town in an image confirming to the romanticized views of exotic places held by the British colonialists.

Fig 1.15: Peace Memorial Museum

Formation of the Segregated City

In the early years of British rule, the organic growth and densification process of Zanzibar Town continued unabated and in an unchanged fashion on both sides of the creek. The whole of Ng'ambo as it is known today was urbanized by the middle of 1920s, as the 1927 town survey shows. In the 1930s, a system of racial segregation based on ethnic divisions between Africans, Arabs, Europeans and Indians was imposed on the area turning it into a typical colonial African city.

The contours of the racial zoning that was established followed the line of the creek, as can be seen in the plan drawn by Lanchester in 1923. The western half of town was reserved for the elite of European, Arab or Asian descent, whereas Ng'ambo was designated as 'native quarters'. An exception was made for the area just east of the creek, which was, at the time, already largely settled by the community of Khoja Indians. The colonial government succeeded in creating a dual city. The divisions and distinctions made between the two parts of the city were founded on a number of seemingly homogenous and clearly defined categories and classifications. Efforts to fix racial boundaries were sustained, among others, by attempts to associate building types and materials with race. The legally defined 'hut' was, for instance, associated with Africans and banned from Stone Town.

Although the reality was far more intermixed than the neat lines on the map would suggest, turning the creek, a natural barrier, into a *cordon sanitaire* did, in the long run, affect the social life of the inhabitants. Until the introduction of racial segregation, people participated in cultural and political activities on both sides of the creek. From the 1930s onwards, 'crossing over' from one side to the other to take part in the cultural life of town became less and less frequent.[15] However, a great number of day-labourers continued to commute to Stone Town on a daily basis.

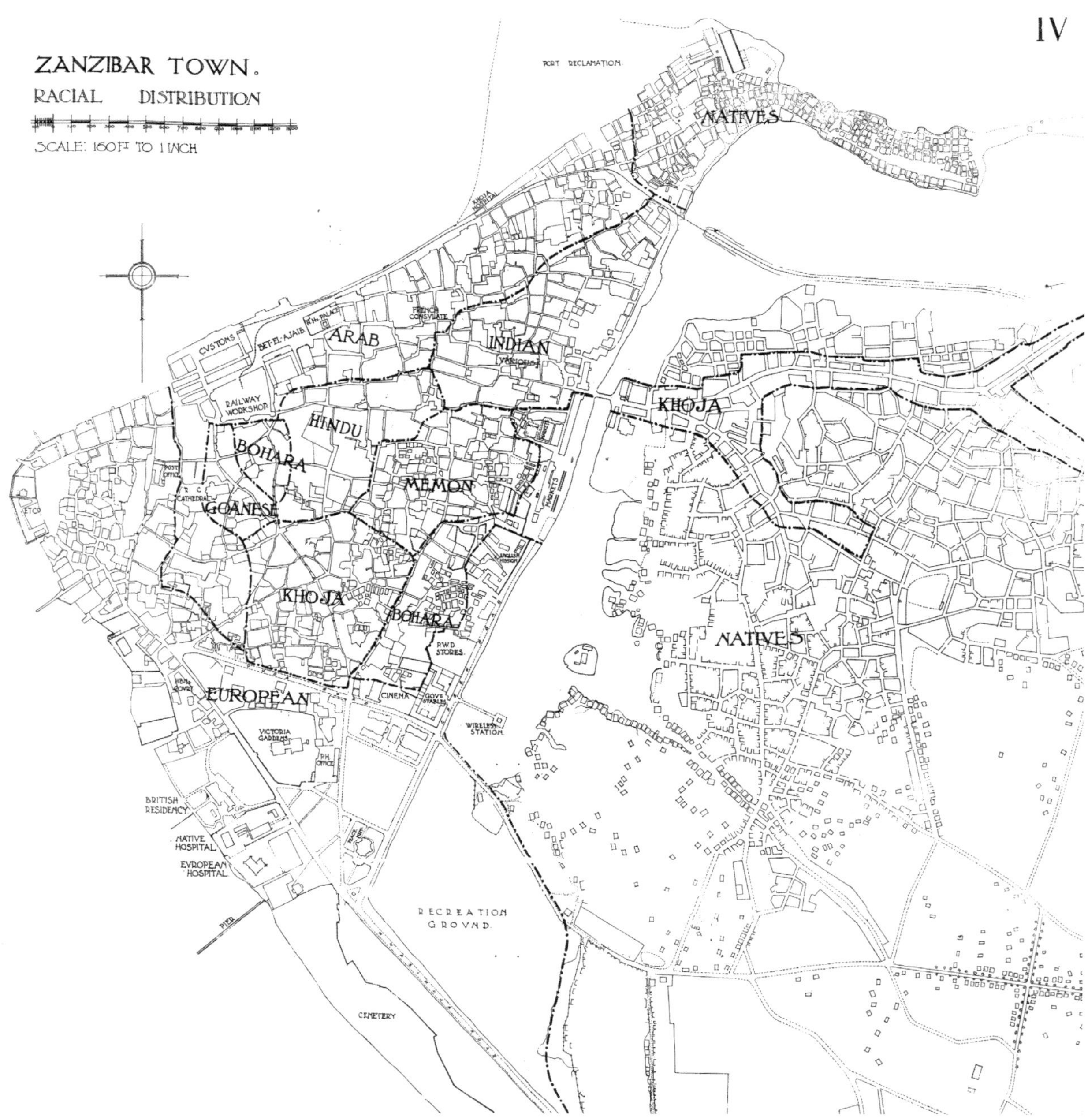

Fig 1.16: Zanzibar Town. Racial Distribution by H.V. Lanchester

15 Laura Fair, *Pastimes and Politics: Culture, Community and Identity in Post-Abolition Urban Zanzibar, 1890-1945* (Ohio, Ohio University Press, 2001), p. 21.

Over the years, regulations were drafted and administered separately for the dwellings and structures on either side. Surveys carried out by the colonial administration in the late 1920s and late 1950s, as well as by the post-independence master-planners in the late 1960s, often dealt with cadastral disputes and compensation issues, paving the road to the overall rehabilitation of Ng'ambo. The 'native quarters' were considered a disorganised slum, whose only chance lay in the complete replacement of the existing building stock. Notwithstanding the quality of its housing and public realm, an overall rationalisation of the urban tissue devoid of any cultural drivers was considered the only possible solution for Ng'ambo. The theoretical split dividing the city into *Stone Town* and the *Other Side* with their own set of rules and plans has survived up to the present and was further reinforced by designating Stone Town as a World Heritage Site in 2000.

Fig 1.17: Clearing of the road reserve for the building of the Michenzani blocks, ca.mid-1960s

Zanzibar's town planner Abdul Wahab Allawi commented in 1965 that 80 percent of Ng'ambo's housing stock was of medium to good quality, technically speaking, whereas in the 1961 tourist guide to Zanzibar one can read that Ng'ambo "is by no means at all a slum, being dotted with excellent houses which can earn the pride of proprietorship that is felt by their owners".[16]

[16] Zanzibar Tourist Information Bureau, *A Guide to Zanzibar* (London, The Crown Agencies for the Colonies, 1961), p. 27.

With the declaration of the Protectorate in 1891, the administration of the city was drastically changed by the introduction of a British bureaucratic system. Funds were needed to run the new administration and to support the projected development of Zanzibar into a modern colony. The main source of income was through taxing clove exports, but the abolition of slavery in 1897 caused a crisis in clove production. The freed slaves were reluctant to continue to work on the plantations, and the harvest came under threat. The British administration reacted to the events by imposing land rent and hut tax to motivate the Zanzibari to return to the plantations, in order to secure the harvest and consequently fill the tax coffers. It was claimed that: "Payment of rents would help to induce a work ethic among a population generally perceived as lethargic".[17]

Yet the imposed tax did not work as anticipated. The Zanzibari refused to pay hut tax in rural areas as well as land rent in Ng'ambo, where they had lawfully been living for free on *wakf* land, under the protection of the patron-client system of the Omani rule. The *wakf* lands became a thorn in the flesh of the colonial administration, especially when it was realised that the income produced through *wakf* properties could bring the Crown substantial economic gain.[18] To attain control over *wakf* property, or return it to the realm of private ownership, a British-dominated Wakf Commission was established in 1905.[19] In the following decades, the land in Ng'ambo was gradually commercialized, resulting in a replacement of the traditional patriarchal client-based system by a tenant based-system. This was, to a large degree, achieved through the imposition of ever-increasing ground rents and introduction of new decrees that helped the authorities to secure control over the wakf properties.

One way for the Commission to claim control over *wakf* properties was on the grounds of presumed mismanagement by the *mutawalli*, a senior member of the founder's family or the trustee administrating the land. A famous story in respect to the seizure of the *wakf* land by the British administration concerns the land bequeathed to the people of Ng'ambo by Hamoud Al-Busaidi in the late 19th century. The Wakf Commission, argued that Hamoud's daughter, Jokha binti Hamoud Al-Busaidi, was unable to manage the property because she was a woman. Jokha successfully fought the Wakf Commission until her death in 1922. It was only in 1923, that the property was finally seized, under the pretext that Shawana Al-Busaidi, who inherited the *wakf* from Jokha, had no claim to the *wakf* as she was only the granddaughter of Hamoud.[20]

Jokha's story was recalled in the name of the *mtaa* - Kwa Bijoha (at Lady Jokha's place) - established by the borders of the former *wakf* land. The *mtaa* retained its name until the area was redeveloped under Karume's New Town project in the late 1960s. The sub-division in *mitaa*, inherited by the British, was retained in the land administration and spatial rearrangement of the city. The name '*mitaa*' did, however, gradually disappear from the documents. In the *Ng'ambo Folder* (1948), the old *mitaa* are simply referred to as 'administrative areas'.

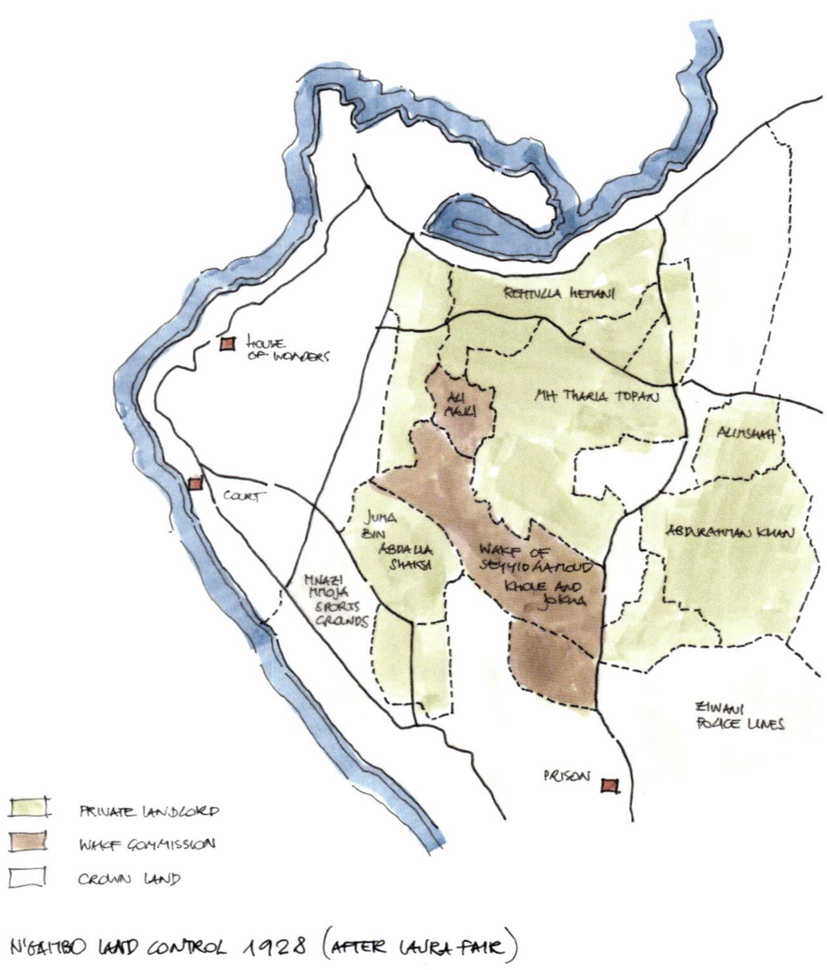

Fig 1.18: Control of land in Ng'ambo ca.1928, drawing after Laura Fair

[17] Laura Fair, *Pastimes and Politics: Culture, Community and Identity in Post-Abolition Urban Zanzibar, 1890-1945* (Ohio, Ohio University Press, 2001), p. 14.

[18] Ibid., p. 125.

[19] Ibid., p. 123. For mcre information on the Wakf Commission, see also: Chapter 3.

[20] Ibid., pp. 125 -128.

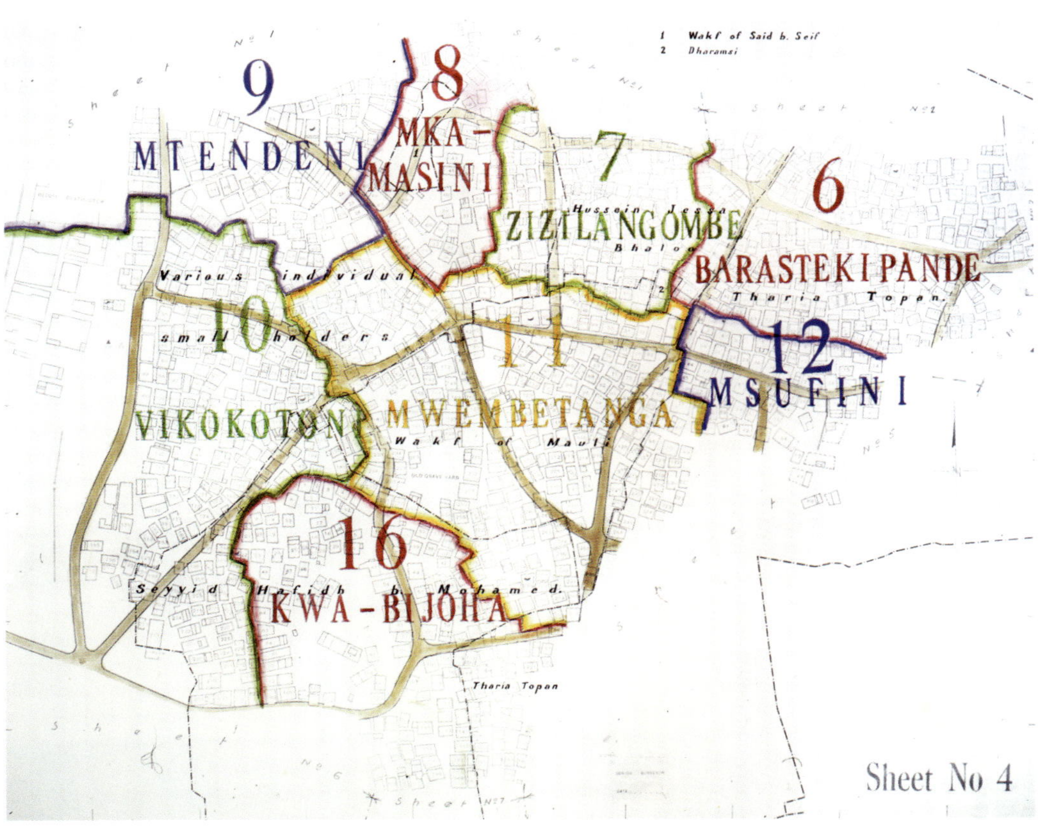

Fig 1.19: *Ng'ambo Folder*: Sheet No.4

British Spatial Planning Exercises in Zanzibar Town

One of the major consequences of the segregation between Stone Town and Ng'ambo in the early years of British colonialism was that most investments in planning and infrastructure went into Stone Town. Piped water, sewage, street lighting, electricity, telephone and paved roads were brought to a reasonable standard in Stone Town but remained only marginally available in Ng'ambo. Eventually, Ng'ambo was to be sanitized and re-planned, as the area was regarded a temporary and unorganised settlement with huts. The attempt to introduce European customs and neighbourhood form to the existing urban environment was made through a heavy-handed system of planning and building controls, through decrees, bylaws and procedures.

Policymaking and planning of urban Zanzibar were far from coherent and consistent. The decrees and planning initiatives enforced by the colonial government were frequently ad hoc, sometimes contradictory and often unrealistic in terms of execution or management, due to chronic shortage of professional personnel and funds. Consequences of colonial bureaucracy and designs can still be felt today. While it is often thought that contemporary problems of the city are a result of postcolonial mismanagement and indigenous incompetence, Bissel suggests otherwise, by pointing to the roots of some of the challenges in the bureaucratic chaos of colonial times.[21]

During the nearly 73 years' existence of the British Protectorate, four integral surveys of Ng'ambo were conducted (1892, 1927, 1936, 1960), an area development dossier created (*Ng'ambo Folder* 1947), and two masterplans were drafted (Lanchester 1923, Kendall-Mill 1958). It is, for this period, a uniquely voluminous and rich collection of urban planning material for East Africa.

[21] William Cunningham Bissell, *Urban Design, Chaos and Colonial Power in Zanzibar* (Indiana, Indiana University Press, 2012), p. 4.

Fig 1.20: Erection of the telegraph pole commonly known as the Wireless in 1921

Lanchester based his *Improvement Scheme for Zanzibar Town* on a short visit to Zanzibar on his way back home from Madras, for which he had prepared a widely recognized master plan. In the scheme Lanchester proposed several interventions for Stone Town including the upgrading plan for the waterfront echoing the Saracenic dreams of Sinclair already mentioned. In addition, he also proposed to build a number of strategic roads through the old fabric, a new harbour, and a replacement of the Swahili houses in Vuga with administrative quarters for European citizens executed in a garden-city manner. The rebuilding of Ng'ambo proposed by Lanchester could only take place on the basis of an integral survey of the area, which would come about after the completion of his *Improvement Scheme for Stone Town*. There were, however, a number of interventions proposed by Lanchester which were implemented irrespective of the survey and have had a lasting impact on the area.

The first, and by far the most important one, concerns the racial zoning borders mentioned before. The second important intervention was the partial filling and formalization of the creek into a canal with a circular tidal basin at the end. This configuration would later become known as the 'Banjo'. Land reclamations enabled a restructuration of the western edge of Ng'ambo with new and straight roads, a railroad embankment, blocks with residences, commercial and public services. Lanchester also proposed to build a residential quarter in the former government quarry, to erect a 'Goanese Village' at the eastern perimeter of Ng'ambo and a public garden at the location of the suburban villa of Mkunguni, or *Kuta la Tembo* (the Elephant House) as it was commonly known. None of these proposals was realized.

VI. Zanzibar Town Improvement Scheme by H. V. Lanchester (1923)

The second survey of Zanzibar Town was carried out following Lanchester's *Improvement Scheme*. It is probably one of the most detailed surveys of the city ever made, and consists of 68 individual sheets (50x90cm) drawn to the approximate scale of 1:500. The map shows the outcome of the interventions proposed by Lanchester: the railway on the northern embankment along Hollis Road and the Banjo, located between Stone Town and Ng'ambo. The suburban parks and villas are still in place along the southern edge of the area. At that moment in time, the two parts of city were already connected by three roads.

It is interesting to note that the majority of buildings found in Ng'ambo today were already in the same location by the 1920s, which indicates that they have continuously been rebuilt on the same footprint for nearly 100 years. The overall pattern of the streets in Ng'ambo has also remained largely unchanged save for the boulevards built by Karume cutting across the urban fabric. The main historical thoroughfares and routes have retained their function and are still in use. The survey work continued throughout the 1930s and was later extended to the whole of Unguja island. In 1936, aerial photographs of the area were taken, which were used to update and refine the 1927 map.

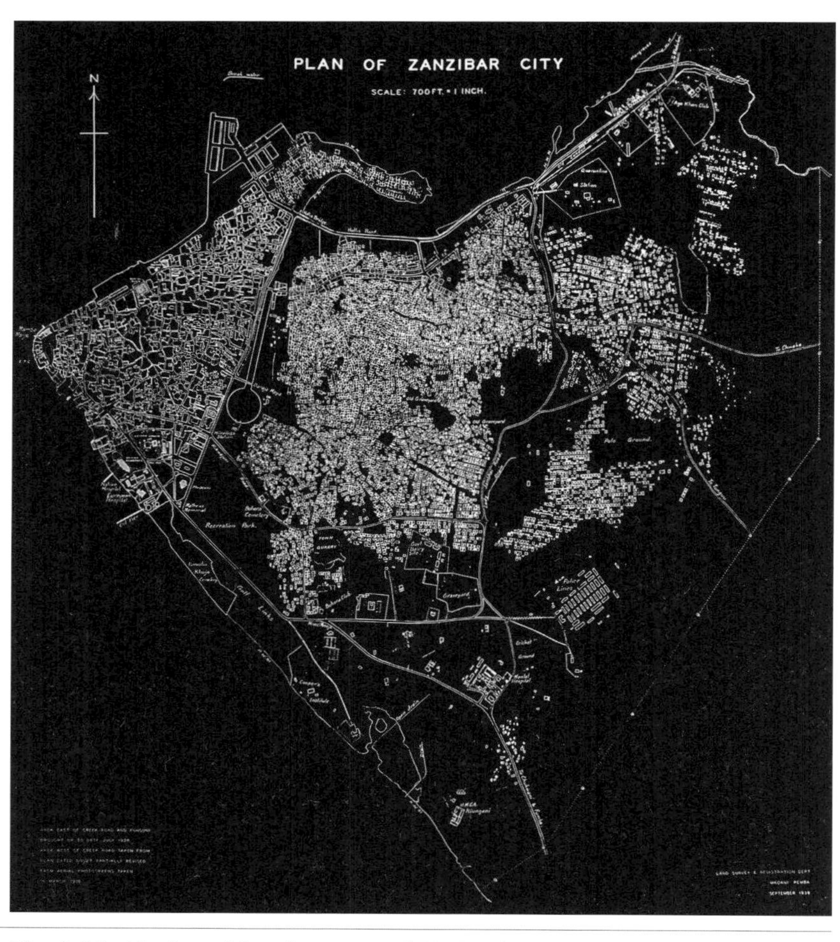

Fig 1.21: Updated land survey of Ng'ambo

Map of Ng'ambo brought up to date in 1938 based on the survey from 1927 and partially revised from aerial photographs taken in March 1936.

VII. Survey of Zanzibar Town (ca.1927)

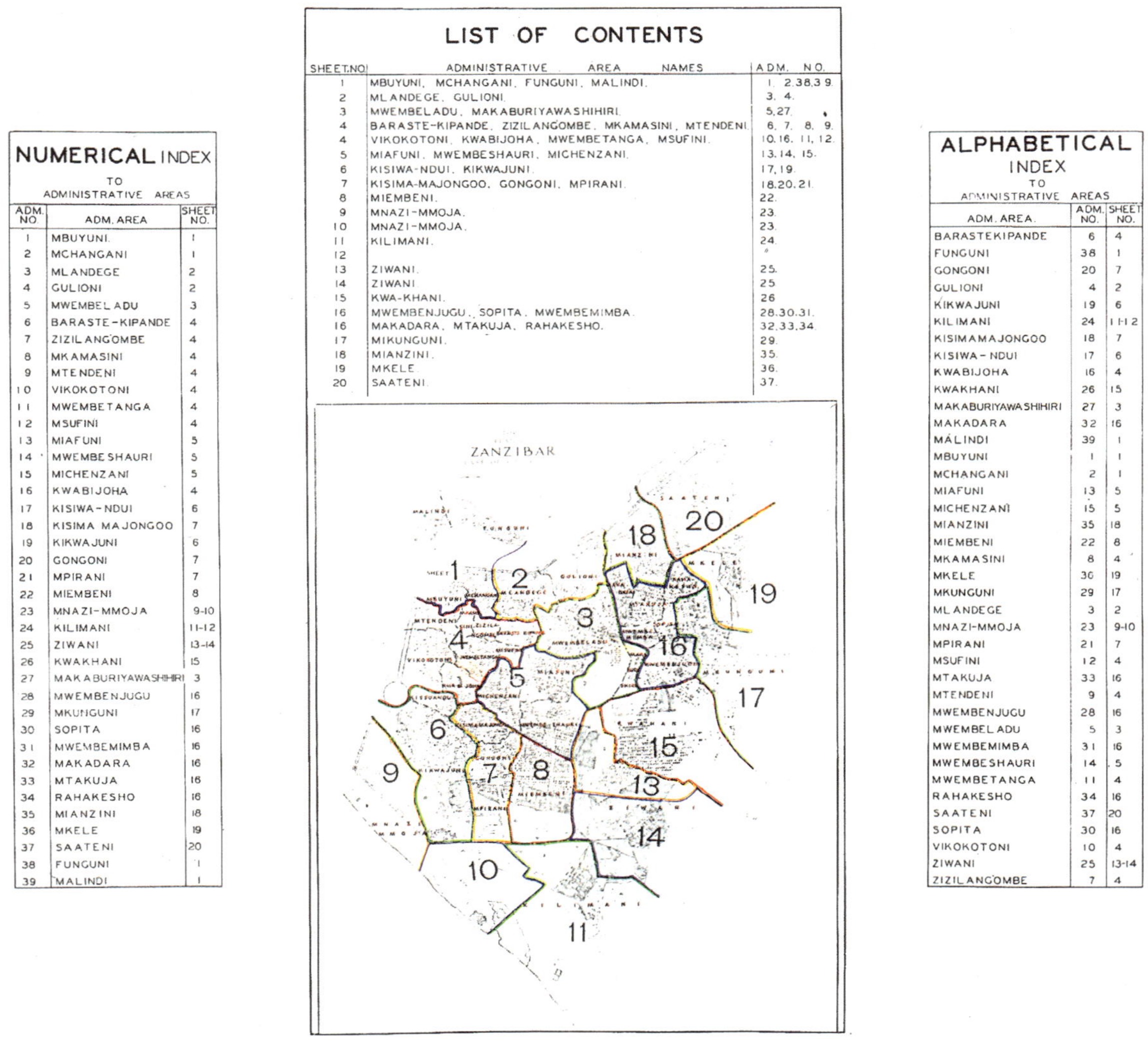

NUMERICAL INDEX TO ADMINISTRATIVE AREAS

ADM. NO.	ADM. AREA	SHEET NO.
1	MBUYUNI.	1
2	MCHANGANI	1
3	MLANDEGE	2
4	GULIONI	2
5	MWEMBELADU	3
6	BARASTE-KIPANDE	4
7	ZIZILANG'OMBE	4
8	MKAMASINI	4
9	MTENDENI	4
10	VIKOKOTONI	4
11	MWEMBETANGA	4
12	MSUFINI	4
13	MIAFUNI	5
14	MWEMBESHAURI	5
15	MICHENZANI	5
16	KWABIJOHA	4
17	KISIWA-NDUI	6
18	KISIMA MAJONGOO	7
19	KIKWAJUNI	6
20	GONGONI	7
21	MPIRANI	7
22	MIEMBENI	8
23	MNAZI-MMOJA	9-10
24	KILIMANI	11-12
25	ZIWANI	13-14
26	KWAKHANI	15
27	MAKABURIYAWASHIHIRI	3
28	MWEMBENJUGU	16
29	MKUNGUNI	17
30	SOPITA	16
31	MWEMBEMIMBA	16
32	MAKADARA	16
33	MTAKUJA	16
34	RAHAKESHO	16
35	MIANZINI	18
36	MKELE	19
37	SAATENI	20
38	FUNGUNI	1
39	MALINDI	1

LIST OF CONTENTS

SHEET NO.	ADMINISTRATIVE AREA NAMES	ADM. NO.
1	MBUYUNI, MCHANGANI, FUNGUNI, MALINDI.	1. 2.38.39.
2	MLANDEGE, GULIONI.	3. 4.
3	MWEMBELADU, MAKABURIYAWASHIHIRI.	5.27.
4	BARASTE-KIPANDE, ZIZILANGOMBE, MKAMASINI, MTENDENI.	6. 7. 8. 9.
4	VIKOKOTONI, KWABIJOHA, MWEMBETANGA, MSUFINI.	10.16. 11, 12.
5	MIAFUNI, MWEMBESHAURI, MICHENZANI.	13.14. 15.
6	KISIWA-NDUI, KIKWAJUNI.	17, 19.
7	KISIMA-MAJONGOO, GONGONI, MPIRANI.	18.20.21.
8	MIEMBENI.	22.
9	MNAZI-MMOJA.	23.
10	MNAZI-MMOJA.	23.
11	KILIMANI.	24.
12		"
13	ZIWANI.	25.
14	ZIWANI	25
15	KWA-KHANI.	26
16	MWEMBENJUGU., SOPITA, MWEMBEMIMBA.	28.30.31.
16	MAKADARA, MTAKUJA, RAHAKESHO.	32.33.34.
17	MIKUNGUNI.	29.
18	MIANZINI.	35.
19	MKELE.	36.
20	SAATENI.	37.

ALPHABETICAL INDEX TO ADMINISTRATIVE AREAS

ADM. AREA.	ADM. NO.	SHEET NO.
BARASTEKIPANDE	6	4
FUNGUNI	38	1
GONGONI	20	7
GULIONI	4	2
KIKWAJUNI	19	6
KILIMANI	24	11-12
KISIMAMAJONGOO	18	7
KISIWA-NDUI	17	6
KWABIJOHA	16	4
KWAKHANI	26	15
MAKABURIYAWASHIHIRI	27	3
MAKADARA	32	16
MALINDI	39	1
MBUYUNI	1	1
MCHANGANI	2	1
MIAFUNI	13	5
MICHENZANI	15	5
MIANZINI	35	18
MIEMBENI	22	8
MKAMASINI	8	4
MKELE	36	19
MKUNGUNI	29	17
MLANDEGE	3	2
MNAZI-MMOJA	23	9-10
MPIRANI	21	7
MSUFINI	12	4
MTAKUJA	33	16
MTENDENI	9	4
MWEMBENJUGU	28	16
MWEMBELADU	5	3
MWEMBEMIMBA	31	16
MWEMBESHAURI	14	5
MWEMBETANGA	11	4
RAHAKESHO	34	16
SAATENI	37	20
SOPITA	30	16
VIKOKOTONI	10	4
ZIWANI	25	13-14
ZIZILANG'OMBE	7	4

Fig 1.22: *Ng'ambo Folder*: List of Contents

A new period of colonial involvement in spatial planning of Ng'ambo commenced with the appointment of Eric Dutton, a colonial official well-known in Eastern Africa, as chief secretary (second in command) in Zanzibar. In 1943, Dutton launched a comprehensive scheme to reconstruct Ng'ambo as a modern, popular suburb. The plan drafted by Dutton was the most expensive and ambitious state intervention in the area until the 1964 revolution, and it was the first time that a plan encompassing Ng'ambo in its entirety was made. As a part of the planning process Ng'ambo was organised into a set of 40 administrative units, presented on 20 separate sheets and grouped under the title *Ng'ambo Folder*. Apart from providing information on land ownership and administrative boundaries, the sheets also included a few planning proposals such as reservations for public facilities on government land and indications of future roads. In the end, the *Ng'ambo Folder* served the colonial officials to control the development of Ng'ambo as far as rebuilding or extension of buildings was concerned, but little was realized of the projected road reserves.

Dutton's post-war comprehensive redevelopment programme, aimed at the remaking of Ng'ambo into a shining example of a new African Welfare State, included interventions into the area on various levels of urban scale: the individual building, neighbourhoods and the entire area. The most significant of them was the construction of the Civic Centre at Raha Leo ('Happiness Today'), which was to become the radiating heart of Ng'ambo from which modern civilization would be spread.

Fig 1.23: Civic Centre in 1961

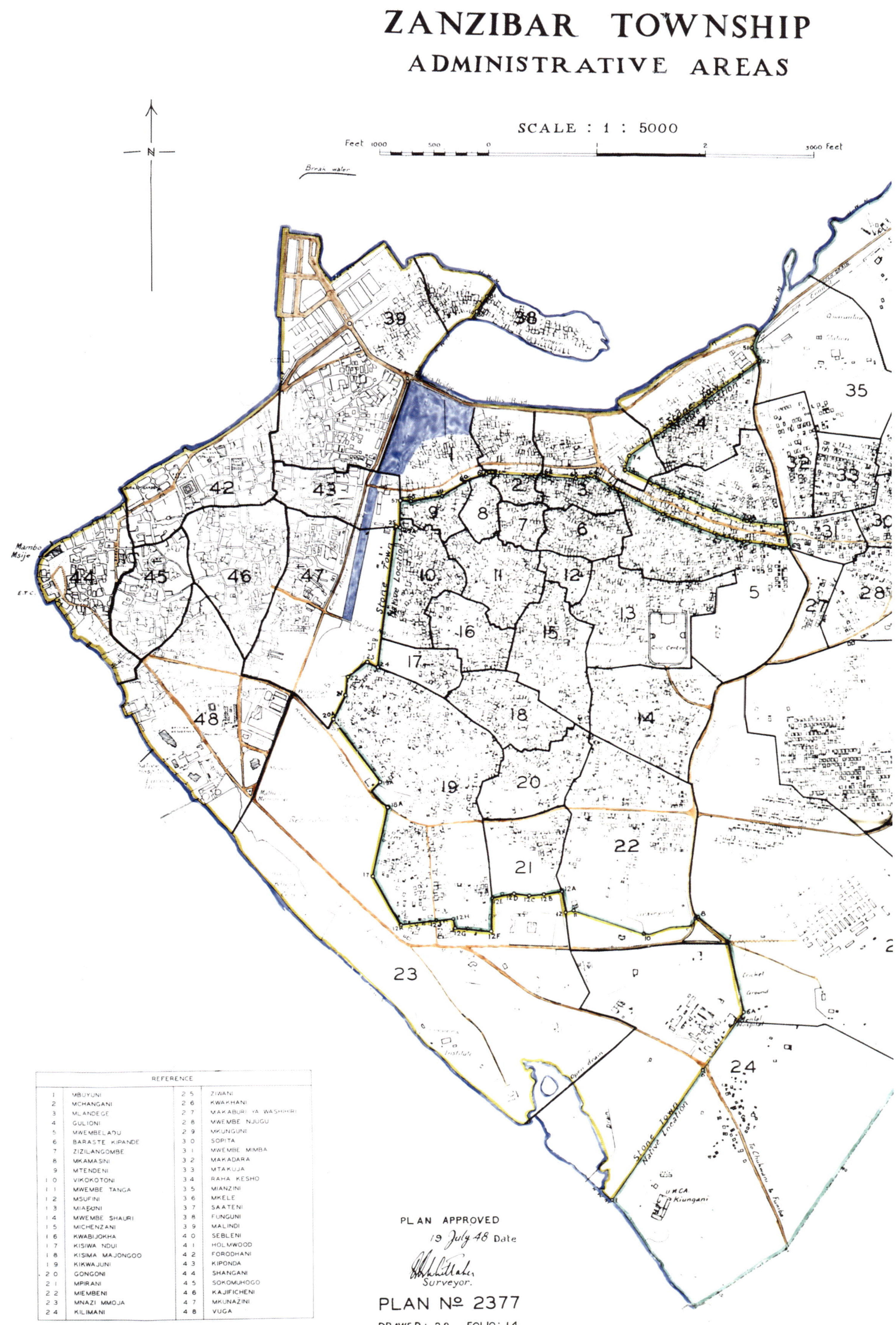

VIII. Ng'ambo Folder (1947)

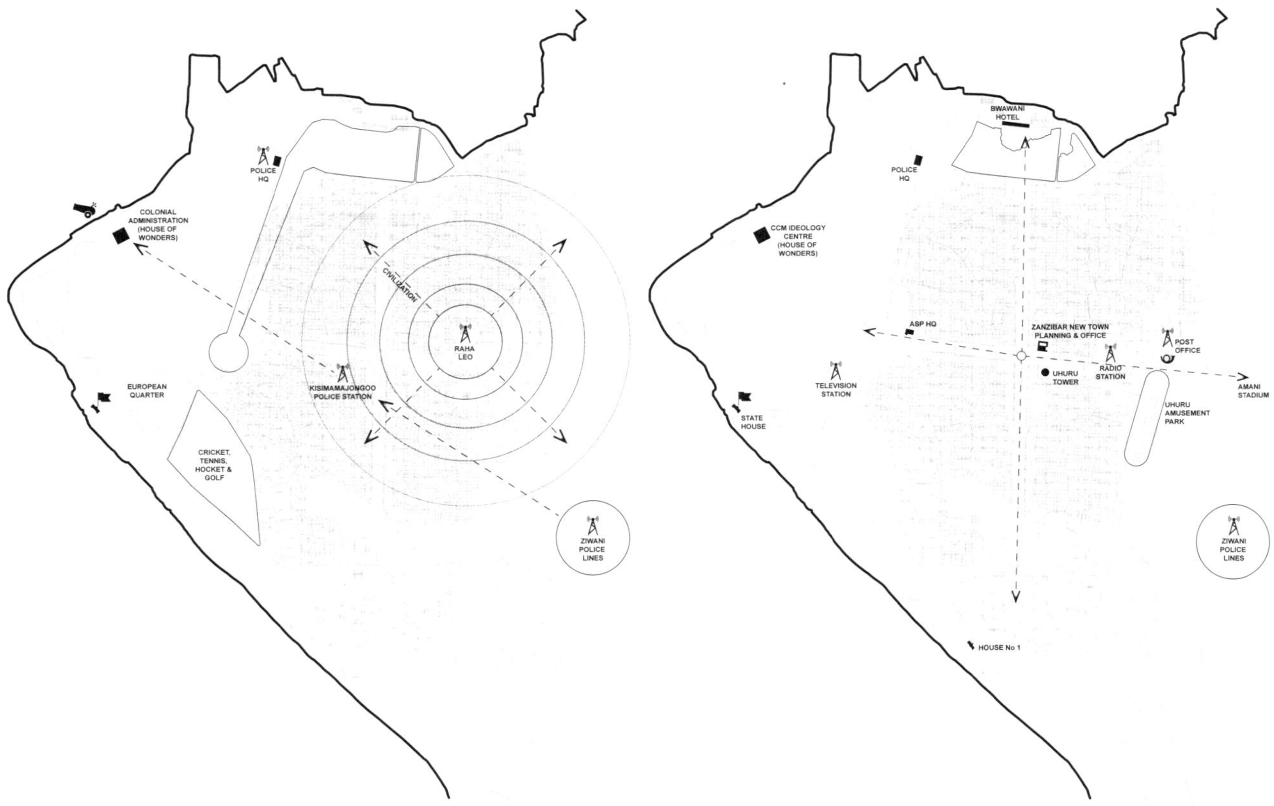

Fig 1.24: Colonial and post-colonial vectors of government control

The late-colonial control mechanism (left), radiating from inside out, was superimposed on an earlier system that consisted of linear control vectors, crossing Ng'ambo from the outside inwards. An example of such a control vector was the signal line starting from the Police Lines at Ziwani, east of Ng'ambo, picked up at Ng'ambo Police Station in Kisiwandui and transferred to the House of Wonders, the seat of colonial administrative power. At the beginning and end of the working day, the siren signal from Ziwani would reach Ng'ambo Police Station, from which another siren called the House of Wonders, where a cannon was shot. This was a signal for the day-labourers to return to their homes in Ng'ambo. The revolutionary control mechanism (right) is manifested in the Michenzani crossroads that creates the two main axes cutting through the city: the East-West Axis with the ASP Headquarters and Television Station in the west (via the New Town construction office and Raha Leo to the Central Post Office and Uhuru Fun Fair in the east); and the North-South Axis from Bwawani Complex and Conference Centre in the north (via the New Town construction office to the residences of the main party members and the president's residence (House #1) in the south). Meanwhile, the above described old colonial police line of control from Ziwani to the House of Wonders remained intact.

Fig 1.25: Ajit Singh

Fig 1.26: Eric Dutton

Images 1.27-1.32:

As a part of the gradual reconstruction of Ng'ambo the government planned and implemented a number of smaller projects. One of them was the provision of low-cost housing schemes and model neighbourhoods that were to replace what was considered an unorganised urban tissue.

Standard housing models, called 'utility houses' because of the role they played in the redevelopment of the area, were designed by the Zanzibari architect working at the Department of Public Works, Ajit Singh. The houses were built on neat orthogonal street grids in the neighbourhoods of Gulioni, Mwembetanga and Miembeni (Mjimpya).

Other, small scale and specific projects that were initiated by the government in this period encompassed the Banjo Park and the children's playground in Mwembetanga. The Banjo Park, today called Jamhuri Park, was created on the location of the circular pond at the end of the tidal canal, which was filled up at about this time. The playground at Mwembetanga would become known as Mapembeani, meaning 'at the big-swings'. The Mapembeani project also encompassed the rebuilding and paving of the surrounding streets with 'utility houses'.

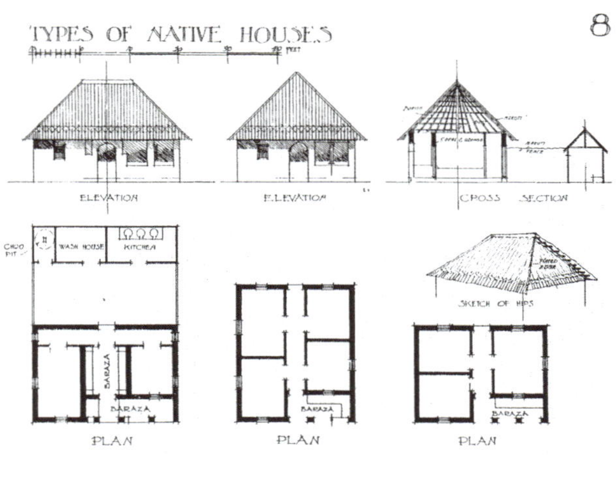

Fig 1.27: Proposed standard low-cost houses design for Ng'ambo by H.V. Lanchester (1923)

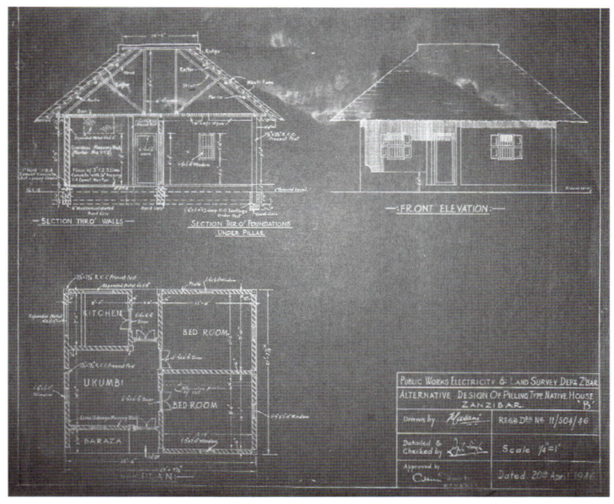

Fig 1.28: Utility houses by Ajit H. Singh (1946)

Fig 1.29: Utility houses in Mwembetanga

Utility houses in the post-war reconstruction's model areas were referred to by the names of various colonial officials. The buildings in Mwembetanga were called Wheatley House after the supervisor of native housing.

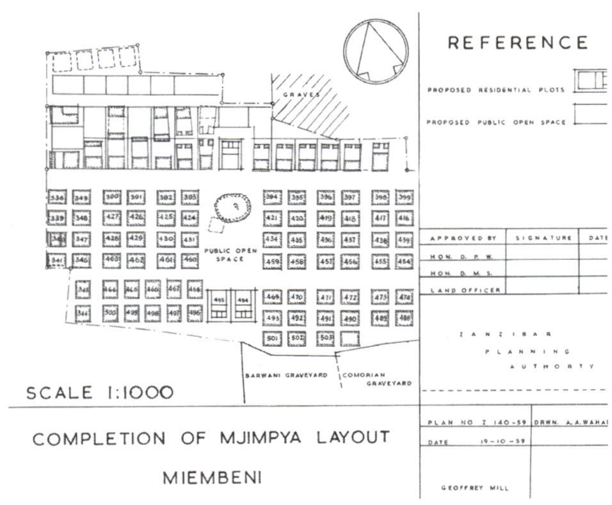

Fig 1.30: Mjimpya layout, Miembeni by Geoffrey Mill (1959)

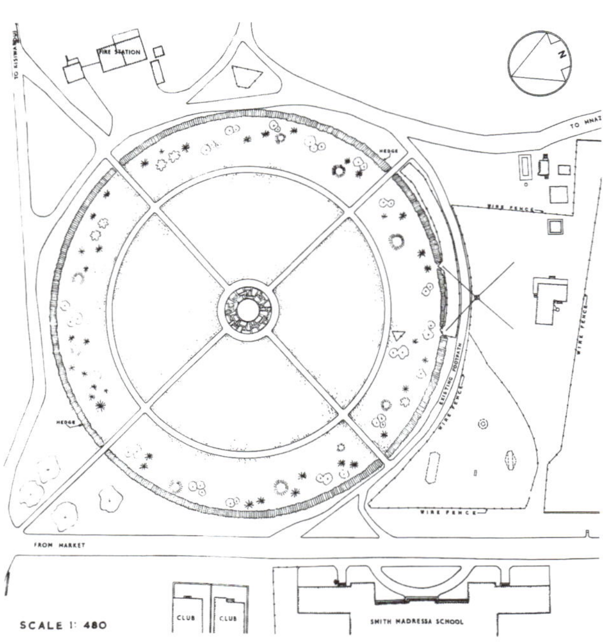

Fig 1.31: Design of the Banjo Park by Geoffrey Mill (1959)

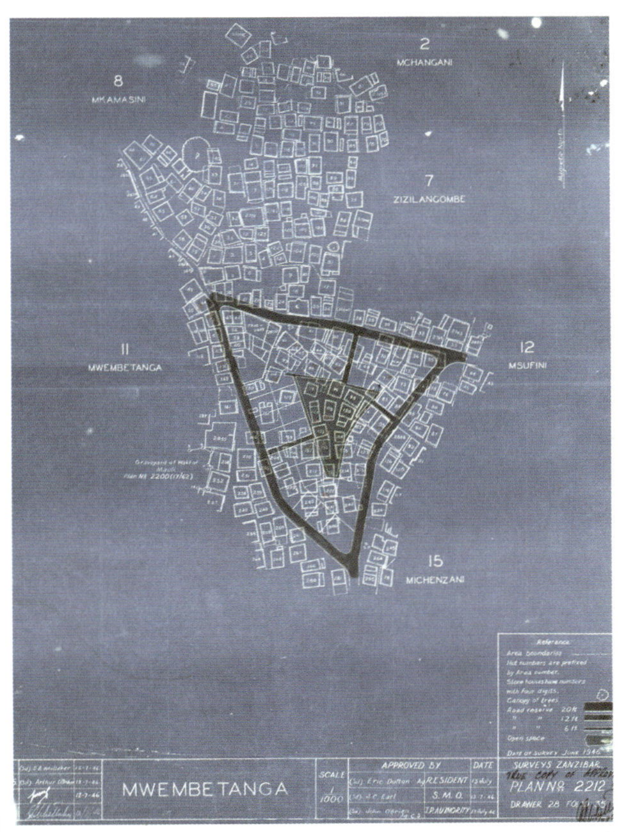

Fig 1.32: Survey and design proposal for the open space in Mwembetanga (1946)

The masterplan of 1958, commissioned to Henry Kendall, was the swansong of British colonial planning activities in Zanzibar. Kendall, seconded by the head of the Zanzibar Urban Planning Department, Geoffrey Mill, drew up a scheme that (re)confirmed the division between Stone Town and Ng'ambo, and defined New Town boundaries to accommodate the growth of the city. The scheme proposed to reclaim the last remnants of the Banjo, and turn it into a green *cordon sanitaire*. It also included the northern area Funguni within the borders of Stone Town and proposed a reclamation of the nearby Bwawani basin for future development.

The Kendall-Mill plan contained little new on Ng'ambo in terms of planning. It restated the protection of government land for public and recreation use, the road reserves outlined in the *Ng'ambo Folder* and the basic zoning division between low-cost residential areas (zone A) in the heart of Ng'ambo and upper-class residences (zone D) in the green and open coastal strip along the southern beaches. Kendall further proposed a reorganisation of Zanzibar Town in semi-autonomous neighbourhood units (NUs) of some 10,000 inhabitants each.

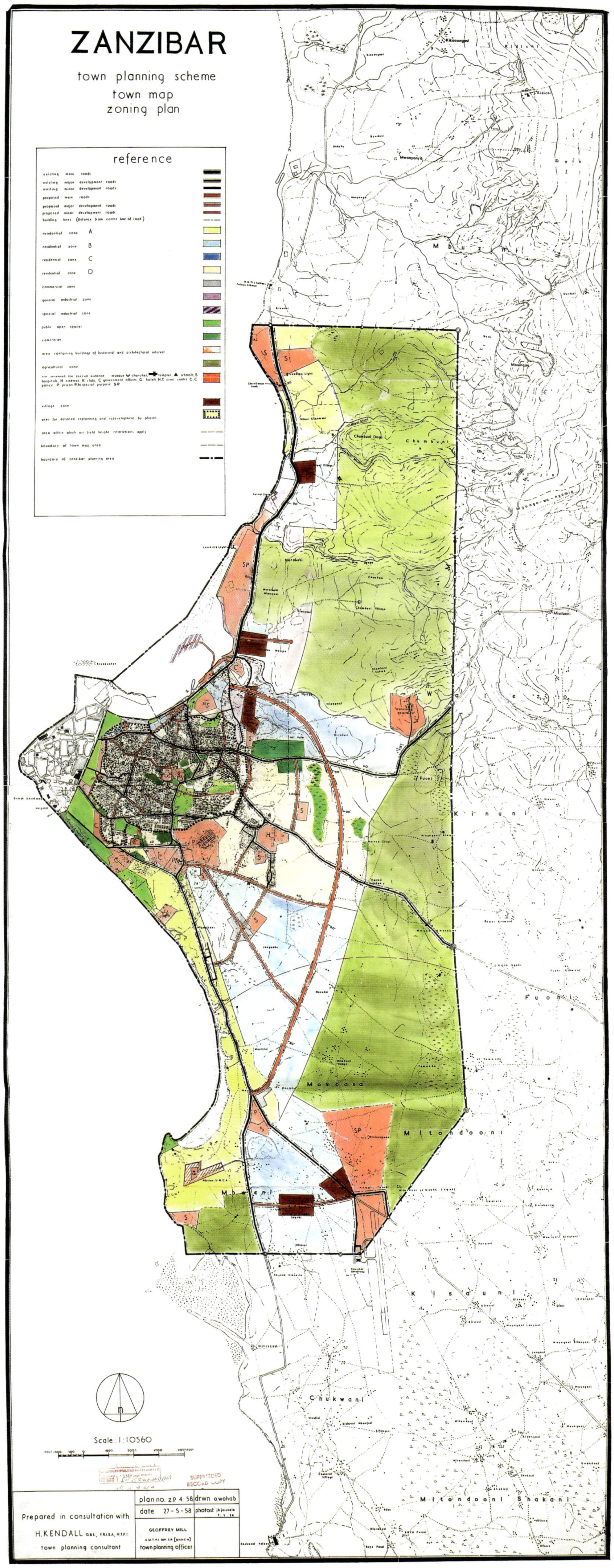

IX. Zanzibar Town Planning Scheme by Kendall-Mill (1958)

Over the years, with its vibrant cultural urban life, Ng'ambo became the setting for day-to-day contestations of the British hegemony in the cultural and spatial realm.[22] A strong voice against the colonial oppression was found in the songs of the famous *taarab* singer Siti binti Saad. But the growing opposition was also manifested in other, less subtle, ways: through political upheavals such as the ground rent strike in 1928. Eventually the area became the backdrop for the 1964 revolution, led by Abeid Karume, himself a resident of Ng'ambo.

Fig 1.33: Kisimamajongoo Sports Club

Fig 1.34: Ndio house

Fig 1.35: Abeid Karume

The house in which Karume grew up and lived at the time of the revolution. The name of the house refers to the word Ndio *(meaning 'yes') followed by the date 1962 on its front gable. According to urban legend this was Karume's way of expressing the inevitable end of the colonial rule and advent of the independence. The Kisimamajongoo Sports Club opposite Ndio house is said to have been an important setting for preparations leading up to the revolution.*

[22] Contestation of the British hegemony in the physical and cultural realm by the inhabitants of Zanzibar Town are investigated in depth by Laura Fair and Garth Andrew Myers in their works on Zanzibar, see bibliography.

Fig 1.36: The umbrella dance

Umbrella dance performed during the Revolution Day celebrations in 1968. Also known as MwanaWaNdege, *the dance was one form of cultural contestation practiced by women of African descent living in the town. It was performed only once a year, on the day of the Sultan's birthday. During the performance, women dressed in clothes and jewellery previously only permitted for Arab people. The umbrella used as an attribute in the performance was, for instance, one of the most important symbolic manifestations of the male ruling class in 19th-century Swahili towns.*[23]

[23] Laura Fair, *Pastimes and Politics: Culture, Community and Identity in Post-Abolition Urban Zanzibar, 1890-1945* (Ohio, Ohio University Press, 2001), p. 106.

Zanzibar Revolutionary New Town (1964-1982)

At the dawn of independence, in 1963, Ng'ambo was primarily a residential area. It was inhabited mostly, but not exclusively, by the working-class and other lower-income groups of African descent. A large concentration of the Indian and Arab population was living along the Darajani-Mlandege artery. Otherwise, the Arab, European and Indian populations were living in Stone Town and on the coastal strip to the south and east of Ng'ambo. By the 1960s, the area was no longer a suburb on the perimeter of the town. The city had expanded to the east, and Ng'ambo naturally became a more central part of it. Nevertheless, in its appearance and structure it remained essentially the same as depicted in the map of 1927, despite the densification and modernization that had occurred. It continued to consist of an extensive organic Swahili urban fabric, dominated by free-standing single-storied Swahili houses.

On 12th December 1963, independence was declared in Zanzibar and the Sultan was installed as the head of a modern constitutional monarchy, not dissimilar from the British model. For a short while it seemed that business would continue as usual in Zanzibar. However, the Arab control over the island strengthened the feeling of alienation among the African majority and only one month later, on 12th January 1964, revolution broke out – to the great surprise of the new rulers. A single-party revolutionary government was formed by the Afro-Shirazi Party (ASP), with Sheikh Abeid Amani Karume (1905-1972) as its president.

The decision to create the Zanzibar New Town was one of the first to be taken by Karume after seizing power. On 8th March 1964, not even two months after the revolution in Zanzibar had started, Karume held an important speech to the population, in which he declared all land to be henceforth owned by the public. He further unfolded his first ideas for a Zanzibar New Town, which incorporated an entire modern city, built on top of and replacing all of Stone Town and Ng'ambo.

Fig 1.37: House No. 4

The southern edge of Ng'ambo comprised a number of suburban villas. One of them was designed by the Tanzanian architect Anthony Almeida, in a modernist style for a rich Indian businessman in 1962. The house was nationalized after the revolution and became the home of the Speaker of Parliament. The house is known in the area as the Speaker's House. No. 4 is a reference to the cadastral number given to the plot after the revolution. Karume's house, located further south, beyond Nyerere Road was given the cadastral number 1.

Fig 1.38: House No. 4, main façade before renovation in 2017

X. Survey of Zanzibar Town (ca.1961)

By the 1960s most of the single-storey Swahili houses that once constituted a large part of Stone Town's tissue had been replaced by Omani houses and Indian shopfront houses, or had given way to the development of the European quarters under Lanchester's scheme. The only part that remained densely built up with single-storey Swahili houses was Funguni, located on the peninsula to the north. The neighbourhood was originally considered a part of Stone Town, but was listed in the 1947 Ng'ambo Folder as 'native quarters'. The neighbourhood, with all of its buildings, was cleared in the 1970s for the development of the Bwawani Complex.

Karume envisioned a New Town that broke with the past. By doing so, not only did he envisage a new socialist city, but also sought to undo the racial split existing between its two parts. It would be a city offering all modern comfort and amenities through the application of cutting-edge technology and modernist planning. To accomplish his vison, Karume had to turn for help to the new allies of the independent Zanzibar: China, Russia, Cuba and the German Democratic Republic (GDR). It would be the GDR, in particular, that saw its chance to realise a tropical socialist utopia. A particular characteristic of Zanzibar New Town is that Karume deliberately opted for his town to replace the existing city, rather than building another town on a greenfield site, as is more usual for New Town initiatives elsewhere in the world.

Images 1.39-1.41:

Prior to commissioning a masterplan for Zanzibar New Town, Karume undertook several pilot projects across Ng'ambo. Starting as early as 1965, two housing schemes with a total of 570 dwellings were developed with the assistance of GDR planners at Kikwajuni and Kilimani. The newly established neighbourhoods were planned to house citizens from Ng'ambo forced to leave their homes to make room for the new city centre. They were eventually filled with party loyalists from outside of the area. The Kikwajuni complex was known among the residents as 'New Berlin Street 'or 'Kikwajuni GDR'. The neighbourhood was also provided with a government-run supermarket, which was closed down in the 1980s.

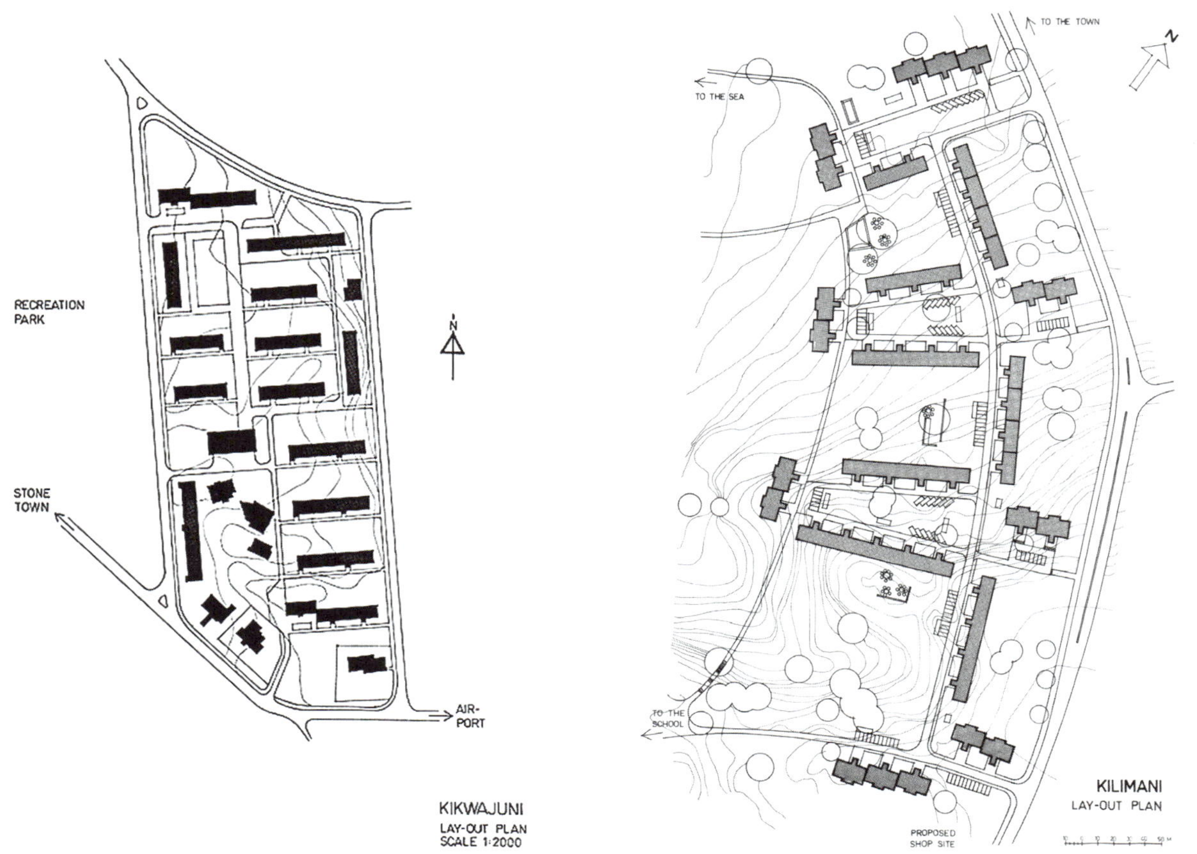

Fig 1.39: Plans of Kikwajuni and Kilimani. After S.Å. Nilsson (1969)

Fig 1.40: Kilimani in the 1970s

Fig 1.41: Kilimani in 2008

Images 1.42-1.44:

During the same period, the new ASP headquarters, Karume's residence (House No. 1), and Bwawani Complex were built in Ng'ambo. These projects formed part of Karume's New Town and can be seen as pilots for the grand scheme that Karume had in mind. Karume strongly believed in modern communication systems. In addition to telephone communication and radio propaganda, he also installed the first sub-Saharan African colour television station in the former Municipal Hall on Creek Road.

Fig 1.42: Afro-Shirazi Party (ASP) Headquarters, now Chama Cha Mapinduzi (CCM) Headquarters

Fig 1.43: Bwawani Complex in 2009

Fig 1.44: Postage stamps, 1974 series

A series of postage stamps issued on the 10th anniversary of the revolution in Zanzibar. They convey the achievements of the revolution: the new Party Headquarters, Zanzibar New Town Housing Scheme, the Amaan Sports Stadium and colour television.

Early Revolutionary Planning: Karume's New Town

In 1966, out of a need to coordinate the various schemes and projects, Karume applied for assistance from the GDR government to draft a new planning scheme for Zanzibar Town. The GDR government, in turn, employed the architect and town planner Hubert Scholz to execute the task in 1967. Scholz worked for the Town Planning Department together with a local team of planners, architects and surveyors headed by the town planner Abdul Wahab Allawi.

The scheme opens with the words: "It is the ardent desire of the Revolutionary Government of Zanzibar to give the people of Zanzibar Town an improvement in the standard of living condition".[24] This sentence sets the tone for the entire project. The overarching aim of the *Zanzibar Town Planning Scheme 1968* was to provide housing for the poor. This was, according to Scholz, a clear distinction from the previous schemes that hardly ever made an effort to improve the living conditions of the 'African People'. It is an aim clearly reflecting the ambitions Karume proclaimed in his 1964 speech.

From the 1968 *Zanzibar Town Planning Scheme*, it appears that the whole of Ng'ambo would be subject to replacement. The masterplan lays out a proposal for a town of 110,000 people and construction of modern-style blocks of flats and houses with all the necessary engineering services such as water and electric supply, as well as public buildings. It also included the construction of a new road system; a new sewerage system not only for storm water but also for waste and soiled water; building of new schools in all residential areas, and concentration of all factories in one or two industrial areas. The plan ignores Stone Town and proposes a structure for Ng'ambo consisting of a new main town centre, three 'major civic centres A' and four 'minor civic centres B' each catering for 10,000 inhabitants, who would be lodged within a radius of 800m or 10 minutes walking distance from the civic centre. As can be seen, Scholz adhered to the same organisational principles as Kendall proposed ten years earlier.

With regard to the infrastructural organisation of the New Town, Scholz proposed a road system of four radial and six concentric main roads, that rationalised the existing road network. All these roads were designed as double carriageways of a total width of a hundred feet (30m). In addition to the four radial access roads, a central spine avenue was projected, designed as the new civic centre for Zanzibar Town. This 'Ng'ambo Centre Road' (now called Karume Road) would connect the television station at the edge of Stone Town via the political ASP Headquarters to the civic centre at Raha Leo. The central axis was designed as a ceremonial way, starting and ending with monuments: one in front of the ASP Headquarters and one in front of what was then the Uhuru Market. However, the central axis was to continue, not as a road but as a greenbelt from Stone Town to the town boundary. Two other green fingers, one along the Funguni creek at the northern shore and one along the botanical gardens and golf course at the southern shore were to connect the city with the countryside.

As far as new housing was concerned, Scholz made a distinction in his plan between multi-storied apartment blocks (located between Creek Road and the outer concentric road) in the western part of Ng'ambo, known as Michenzani, and low-rise terraced and free-standing houses around the perimeter.

[24] Hubert Scholz, *Zanzibar Town Planning Scheme 1968* (Zanzibar, Revolutionary Government of Zanzibar, 1968), p. 1.

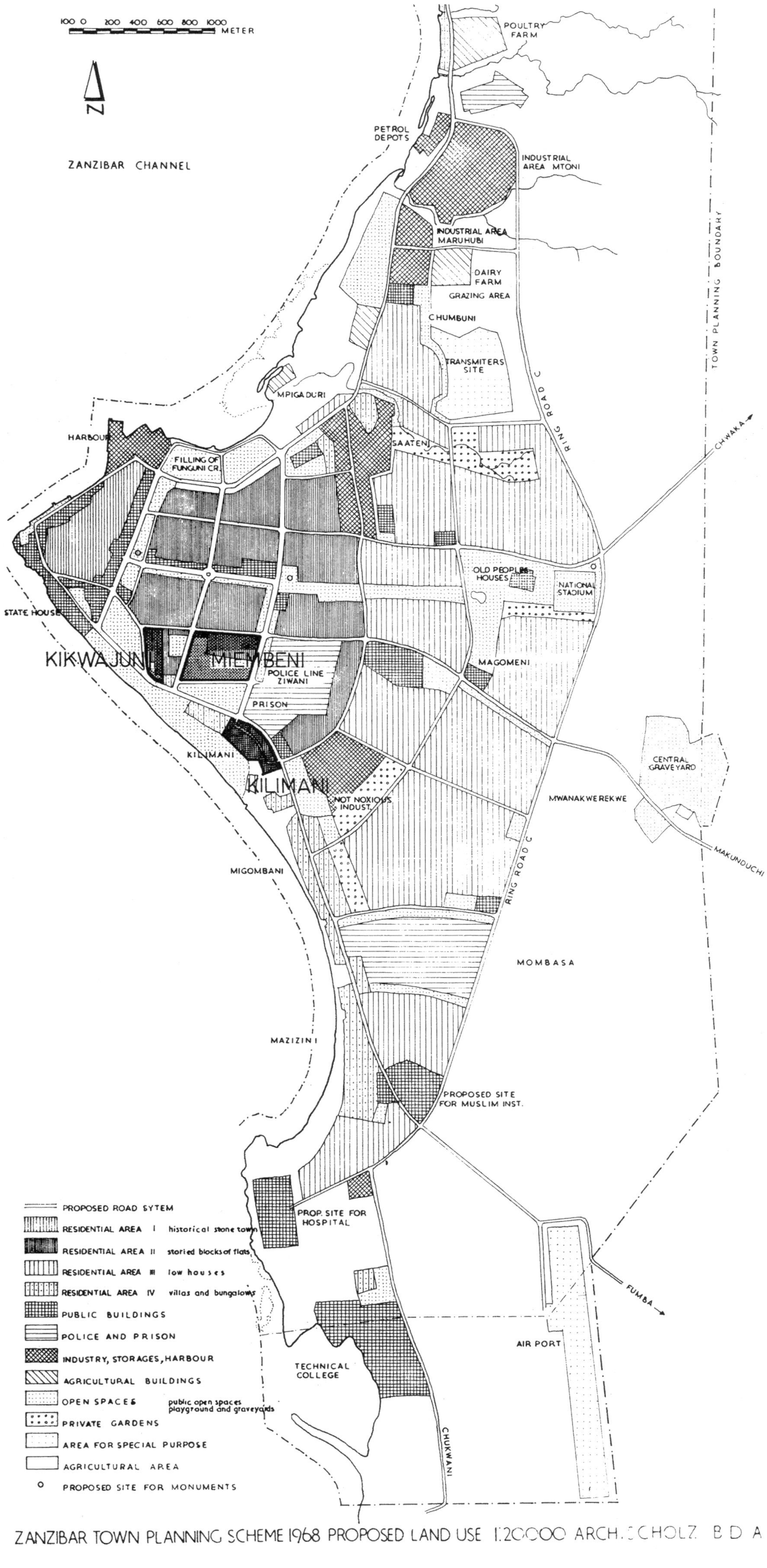

XI. Zanzibar Town Planning Scheme: Proposed Land Use by H. Scholz (1968)

According to Scholz, the monumental Michenzani area was to become the crown on Karume's New Town. The highest apartment buildings in Zanzibar, four to five stories tall, were to be built in the area with some even taller public buildings as landmarks in front of them. These public buildings would house government offices, a new central post office, cinema, polyclinic, main mosque, library, supermarket, shops and restaurants to form the new centre of the city.

However, Karume's personal involvement in the production of the 1968 *Zanzibar Town Planning Scheme* and the consecutive designs of different projects under that scheme cannot be ignored. Scholz left the island for good in 1968 and the involvement of GDR planners and architects in the elaboration and implementation of the plans after that was marginal and did not last much beyond the end of the year.

The work on the New Town was henceforth predominantly in the hands of Karume and the employees of the Town Planning Department, suggesting that it is not so much Scholz, but Karume that should be credited as the main architect behind Zanzibar New Town. One of his major interventions was related to the design of the Michenzani blocks. Karume decided to redesign the boulevards, and instead of continuing with loosely arranged walk-ups, as suggested by the GDR planners, lined them with six- to eight-storied blocks of not less than 300 metres.

Abdul Sheriff has on several occasions referred to the project as the "crucifixion of Ng'ambo". This is not without a reason, since large parts of the Swahili fabric had to make room for the development of the central boulevards cutting through Ng'ambo in due north-south and east-west directions. This Haussmannian intervention could be interpreted in many ways. It could be regarded as a continuation of the colonial need to control the population, or as Ludger Wimmelbücker suggests as a "symbolic triumph over the racially defined inequalities of the past, a clarion call for self-reliance, rendered possible by a new vision of modernity".[25]

Karume's New Town project is unique in its scale and scope in the context of East Africa, and his modernization project went far beyond the lasting imprints it left on the area. Although never fully completed it not only permanently changed the urban fabric of Ng'ambo, but also altered the social life of its inhabitants.

Images 1.45-1.47:

The urban planning strategy of the Revolutionary Government was shaped by a grand vision of which the projects carried out in Ng'ambo were a physical manifestation. Construction of the Michenzani blocks permanently altered the physical and cultural urban environment of Ng'ambo by disrupting the existing neighbourhoods and leading to forced resettlements of the inhabitants. Ironically, it was a building project which would not be completed without obligatory labour being imposed on the local inhabitants.

Fig 1.45: Setting-out plan for new roads and the Michenzani blocks and roundabout (ca.1969-1970)

Fig 1. 46: Construction of the Michenzani blocks

Fig 1.47: Michenzani blocks after completion

[25] Ludger Wimmelbrücker, "Architecture and City Planning of the German Democratic Republic in Zanzibar", *The Journal of Architecture*, 17, no. 3 (2012), pp. 407-432.

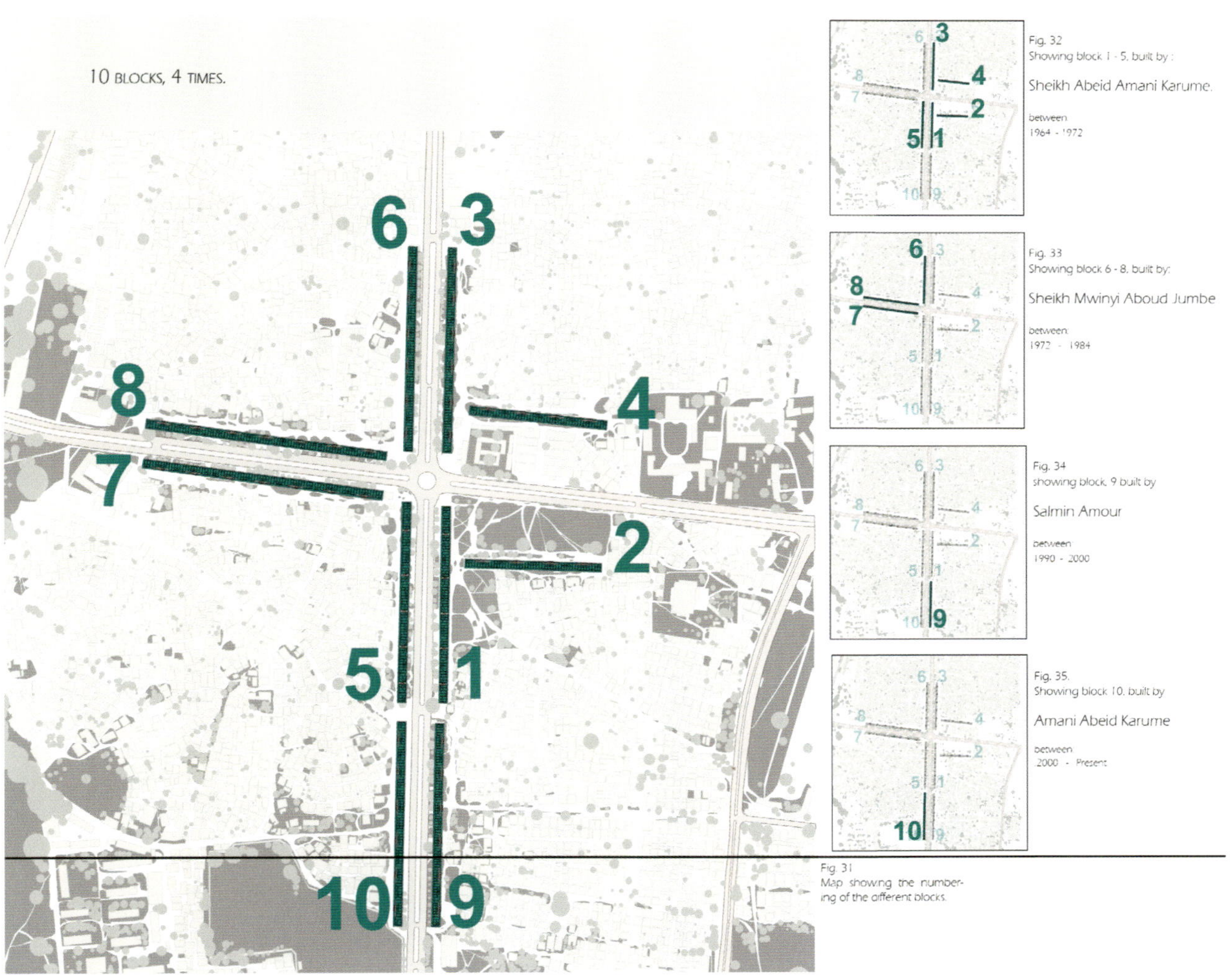

Fig 1.48: Michenzani housing project: stages of construction, drawing by Anna Cornelis

Building of Zanzibar New Town at Michenzani did not stop with Karume's untimely death in 1972. His successors Aboud Jumbe, Salmin Amour and Amani Abeid Karume Jr. continued the construction of the blocks of flats until 2008.

After Karume's untimely death in 1972, parts of his New Town project were realized by his successors. Building of the Michenzani blocks continued in a piecemeal manner until 2008. But it is the children's funfair at the former location of the Uhuru Market, and the Bwawani Complex with a hotel, sports facilities, swimming pools, discotheque and a rowing lake in the Funguni basin (both completed after Karume's death) that are truly revealing of his ambitions to build a comprehensive, modern and emancipated society. These projects, in a sense planned as loose and independent elements, were erected with foreign planning assistance: the Bwawani Complex by the Norwegian architect Nøstvik and unknown architects from Eindhoven, the Uhuru Funfair with Chinese aid. Nøstvik, famous from his Kenyatta Conference Centre in Nairobi, also designed a conference centre at the hinge of Funguni and Malindi, which was, however, not realized.

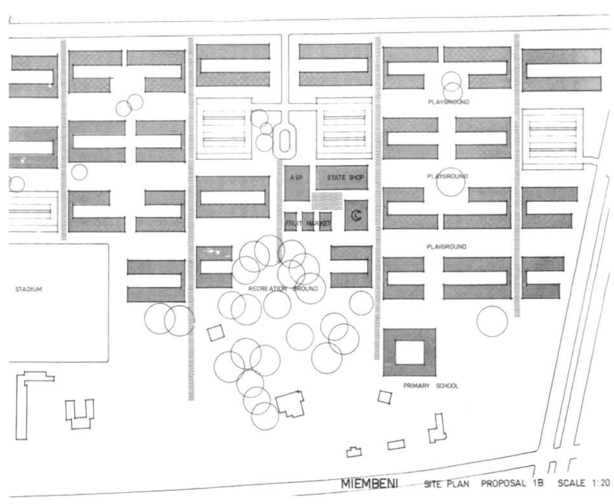

Fig 1.49: Redevelopment proposal for Miembeni by S.Å. Nilsson and B. Lilje of Lund University (1968)

Fig 1.50: Redevelopment proposal for Miembeni by S.Å. Nilsson and B. Lilje of Lund University, sketch (1968)

One of the schemes following the outlines of the 1968 Zanzibar Town Planning Scheme *concerned the redevelopment of Miembeni, an area located south of Michenzani and bordering with Kikwajuni. Redevelopment of this neighbourhood was planned by Swedish experts Sten-Åke Nilsson and Bo Lilje, together with students from Lund University. For Miembeni, Nilsson and his students proposed four alternative plans covering 385 households. In addition, they proposed to convert Miembeni's playing fields, the Mao Tse-Tung Stadium, and the adjoining graveyard into public areas with ample playgrounds, schools and a neighbourhood centre consisting of an ASP branch office, a state shop, market and mosque.*

Fig 1.51: Uhuru Funfair during the opening

Fig 1.52: Funguni-Malindi Conference Centre by Karl Henrik Nøstvik

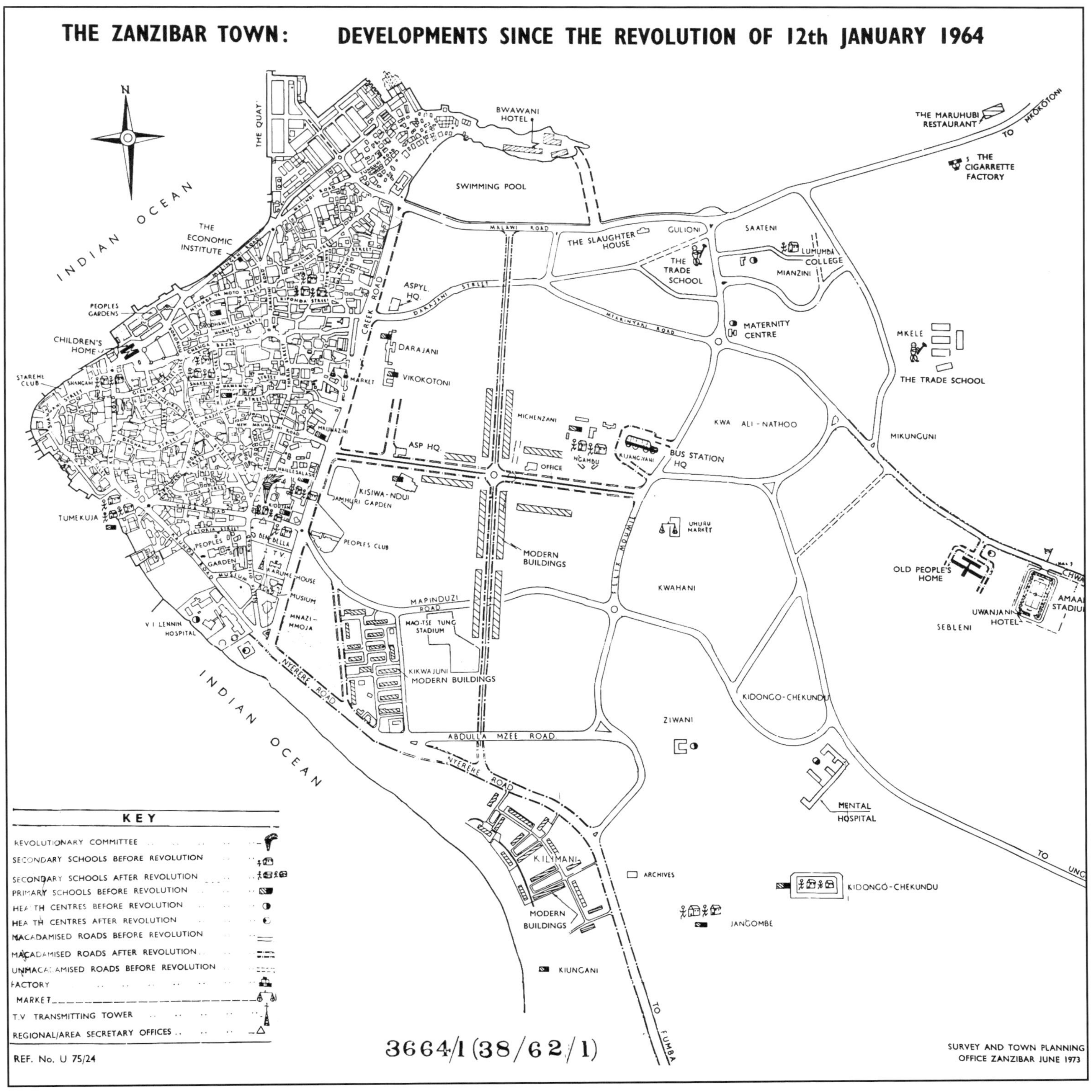

XII. Zanzibar Town: Developments Since the Revolution of 12th January 1964 (1973)

An overview of the achievements of the Revolutionary Government completed between 1964 and June 1973, drawn by Zanzibar Town Planning Office. Note: Karume House (House No. 1) is missing from the map.

Late-Revolutionary Planning

In 1982, the Zanzibar government, presided over by Karume's successor Aboud Jumbe, contracted the Chinese town planners Gu Yu Chang and Qian Kequan to elaborate an update to the 1968 *Zanzibar Town Planning Scheme* for Ng'ambo, as the city was growing beyond its boundaries. By 1982 the city numbered about 200,000 inhabitants, being almost double the amount that Scholz had envisaged in his masterplan. Again, just as Scholz had done, Chang and Kequan excluded Stone Town from their masterplan exercise. The reason for the exclusion, this time, was the increased attention Stone Town received from international conservationists in the 1980s, leading to a number of significant conservation and restoration schemes.

The Chinese planners, seconded by the still active Abdul Wahab Allawi restructured the city into 54 neighbourhood units (NUs). Ng'ambo was divided into four neighbourhood units, NU 1 to NU 4, corresponding with the quarters formed by the Michenzani cross-roads. A new institutional town centre was proposed between Stone Town and Ng'ambo, and a separate cultural and commercial town centre was proposed on the eastern edge of the area, between Raha Leo and Mlandege. The rearrangement of the city into neighbourhood units followed the Arusha Declaration, based on the *ujamaa* ten-cell units, presided over by a CCM party representative. It is notable that the first name on the list of persons consulted for the masterplan was not Zanzibar's president, Aboud Jumbe, but Julius Nyerere, the president of the Union Government of Tanzania.

The 1982 *Zanzibar Town Master Plan* by Chang-Kequan departs from the masterplans of Scholz and Kendall-Mill, structured on modernist neighbourhood units intended for 6,000-10,000 inhabitants each. Chang-Kequan reduced the neighbourhood units to some 2,000 inhabitants each, thereby accommodating them to the size of the *mtaa*, the original 'neighbourhood unit' of Zanzibar Town. In relation to Ng'ambo, Chang-Kequan also broke with Scholz and Karume's ideas to replace the Swahili urban tissue with a complete new, modernist fabric. Instead, they returned to the approach suggested in the *Ng'ambo Folder* of 1947, which foresaw a gradual reconstruction of Ng'ambo on the existing pattern, but with widened reserves for strategic roads.

***

The development of Zanzibar New Town was a traumatic experience for many residents of Ng'ambo. Older inhabitants refer to the revolution as a main turning point in the cultural life of the area. In the course of the Ng'ambo Tuitakayo research, there was little time or capacity available to gather substantial data on the developments in dance, music and performance that took place between the revolution and the present day. The reluctance of people to discuss the period following the revolution has resulted in an image of the area that primarily reflects cultural life from before the revolution. Nevertheless, Ng'ambo remained a key area for sports and recreation throughout the years. The former town stone quarry at Kikwajuni was converted into the Mao Tse-Tung Stadium during the early days of revolution, but would lose its strategic importance to the Amani Stadium east of Ng'ambo in the late 1960s. Otherwise, new *taraab* groups and music bands were emerging, while the cultural life was slowly moving from the streets to new venues such as hotels (*see* Chapter 2, pp. 116-124).

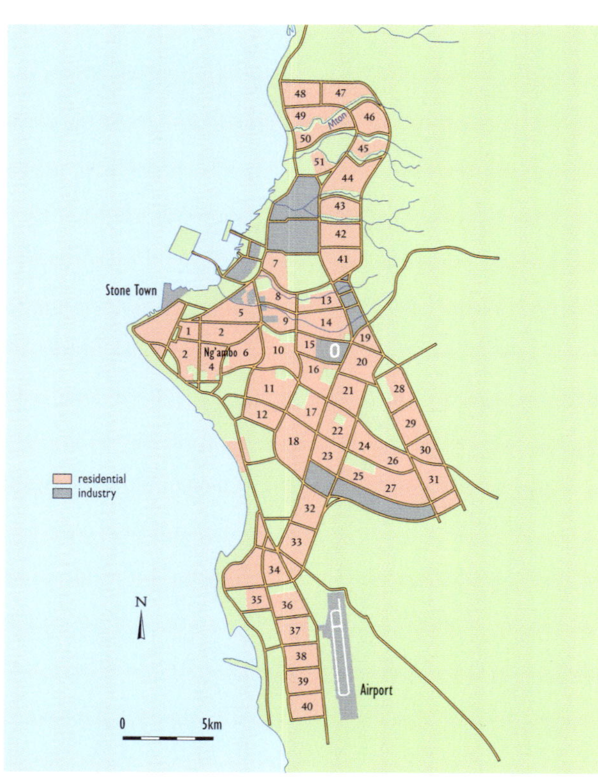

Fig 1.53: Zanzibar Town Master Plan by Chang-Kequan (1982)

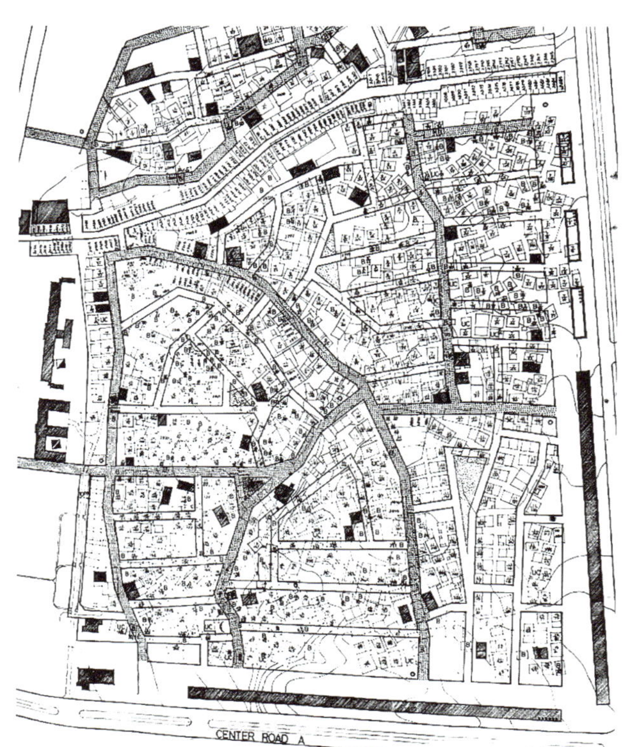

Fig 1.54: Mwembetanga redevelopment proposal by Chang- Kequan (1982)

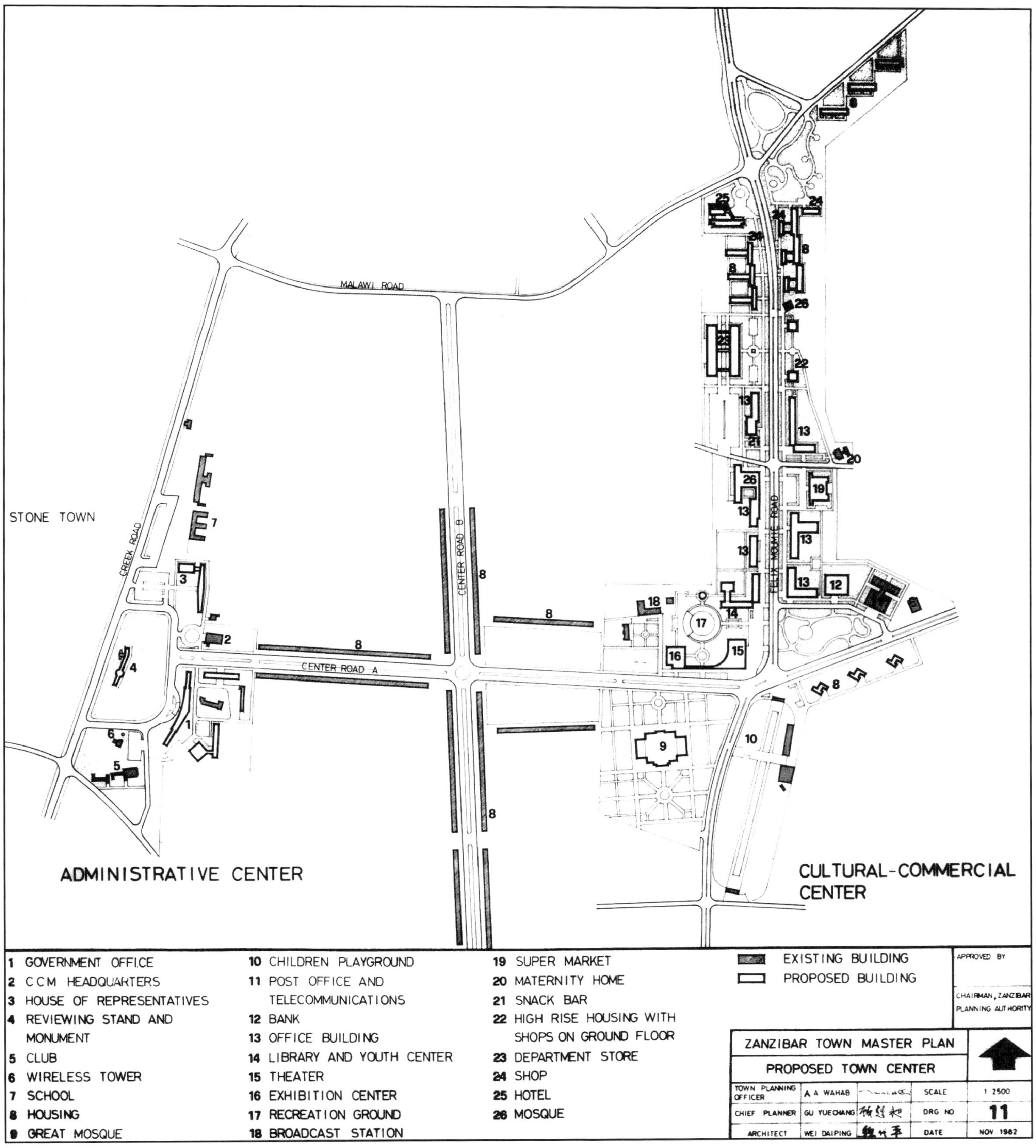

XIII. Zanzibar Town Master Plan: Proposed Town Center by Chang-Kequan (1982)

The Organised Disorder - Spatial Organisation of Ng'ambo

The repeated attempts to redevelop the area by the colonial and post-colonial governments might suggest a lack of planning rationale behind the existing Swahili urban tissue in Ng'ambo. However, there is nothing more deceiving for an uninformed and perhaps and unwilling eye than the 'organised disorder' of the area. According to Myers, the communities in Ng'ambo are both ideologically and practically built on three cornerstones: *uwezo* 'power', *imami* 'faith' and *desturi* 'custom', which have shaped the urban tissue of the area. The three cornerstones mentioned by Myers are manifested on all planning levels, starting with the design of individual buildings, their arrangement in relation to each other, and extending to the form of the neighbourhoods.

Uwezo can be translated, depending on the context, as capability, wealth, status or power, and is frequently used in relation to the built form reflecting the intimate connection between visible physical wealth and the less tangible social power. In colonial times, the *uwezo* of house owners was primarily manifested in a building's permanency. Today, the *uwezo* can be seen in the improved conditions of the respective buildings, use of cement blocks, as well as the continuous upgrading made to the individual homes which Myers also credits to the *desturi* of perfectionism present in the area.

Back in the day, the *uwezo* of an owner was effectively translated into her or his position in the existing power-relations matrix, setting the general parameters for the quality and durability of one's house, and for its location in the city. This created an urban landscape largely moulded on the sociocultural and economic hierarchy of the inhabitants in the respective *mitaa*. Historically, the well-to-do areas were located in the north-west with the overall condition of neighbourhoods declining towards the east. Based on the field work from 1996, Myers notes that the physical quality, architectural complexity, and level of adornment of houses declines with a move eastward, which confirms that the historical spatial-hierarchy is maintained in the area. These findings have been further confirmed by the Ng'ambo Tuitakayo field survey.[26]

Fig 1.55: View from the rooftops of Michenzani blocks

Fig 1.56: View from the rooftops of Michenzani blocks

26 Information in this section is based on the reading of spatial order in Ng'ambo proposed by Garth Myers in Garth Andrew Myers, *Reconstructing Ng'ambo: Town Planning and Development on the 'Other Side' of Zanzibar*, PhD (Los Angeles, University of California, 1993), in particular pp. 134, 165, 446; Garth Andrew Myers, "Sticks and Stones: Colonialism and Zanzibari Housing", *Africa*, 67, no. 2, (1997), pp. 252-272.

Laissez Faire and World Heritage Site (1982-2014)

Completion of the 1982 Chang-Kequan masterplan marked the end of an era. Of all the ambitious proposals put forth over the years for Ng'ambo, hardly anything materialized. Nothing came of the envisaged rehabilitation of the four NUs of Ng'ambo either. No investments were made in infrastructure and roads, while water supply and drainage fell into a serious state of disrepair. Private initiatives in Ng'ambo were scarce as the economy of Zanzibar was in decline and the residents were reluctant to invest in the area, fearing imminent eviction after the shock caused by the New Town developments in the 1960s and 1970s.

Following the revolution, Zanzibar Town went through a profound social transformation, which affected, in particular, the building stock of Stone Town. Many of the nationalized properties were abandoned by former urban dwellers, who were replaced by rural families often without means to maintain the stone houses. The neglect of Stone Town in the ensuing years grew to such an extent that frequent collapses and demolitions occurring in the 1980s, rousing an alarm among conservationists, followed by the subsequent interest of global players such as the United Nation Centre for Human Settlement and UNESCO (1982-1984).

XIV. Ordinance Survey (1985)

During the 1980s, a new urban segregation arising from the colonial past started to take root. It was first formalized by omitting Stone Town in the 1982 Chang-Kequan masterplan. The next step was the creation of an independent Stone Town Conservation and Development Authority in 1985 (STCDA received its legal status in 1994) and drafting a separate conservation scheme for Stone Town in 1996, which eventually led to its inscription on the UNESCO World Heritage List in 2000. By the declaration of Stone Town as a UNESCO World Heritage Site, Ng'ambo, once again, became 'the Other Side', clearly separated from Stone Town by Creek Road. The two western quarters of Ng' ambo were designated as the buffer zone to the World Heritage Site, which effectively means that any future developments in these areas are conditional on the interests of Stone Town.

Although the thirty years between the early 1980s and early 2010s can be described as a time of decay and laissez faire in Ng'ambo, it was not completely void of development. Apart from the piecemeal construction of the Michenzani blocks, the Town Planning Department developed ideas for the conversion of the 'scar tissue' around them into a city park in 1991. The department also made detailed plans in the 1990s for the development of the cultural-commercial town centre around Mlandege, as suggested in the 1982 masterplan. The first commercial 'high street' buildings began to appear in the area by the end of the 20th century, a radio station was built in front of the Civic Centre in Raha Leo and a large Friday Mosque was erected on the location suggested in the 1982 masterplan.

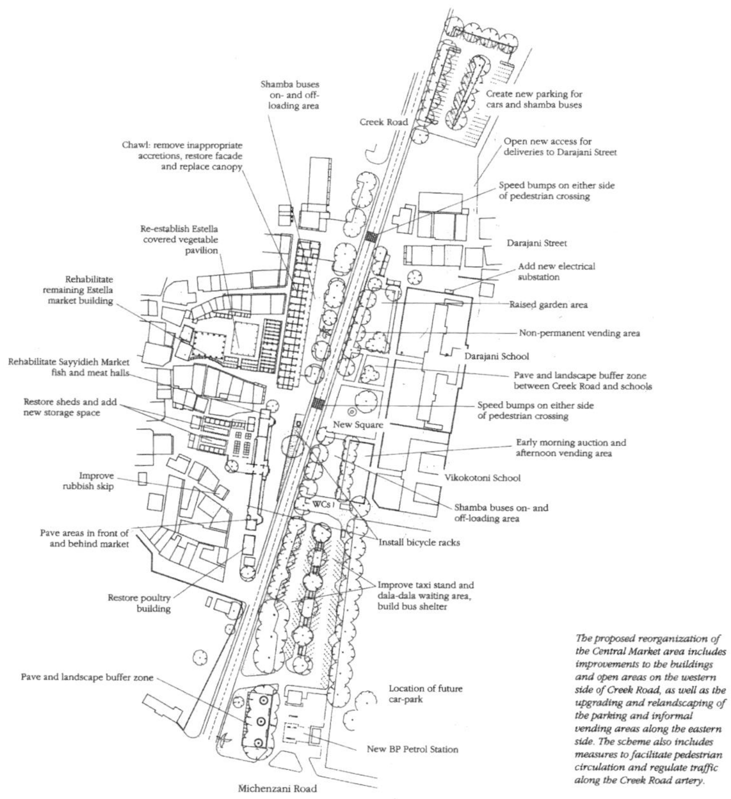

Fig 1.57: Site plan of the proposed reorganisation of the central market (Darajani Market) (1996)

The plan proposed an improvement and upgrading of public facilities and spaces.

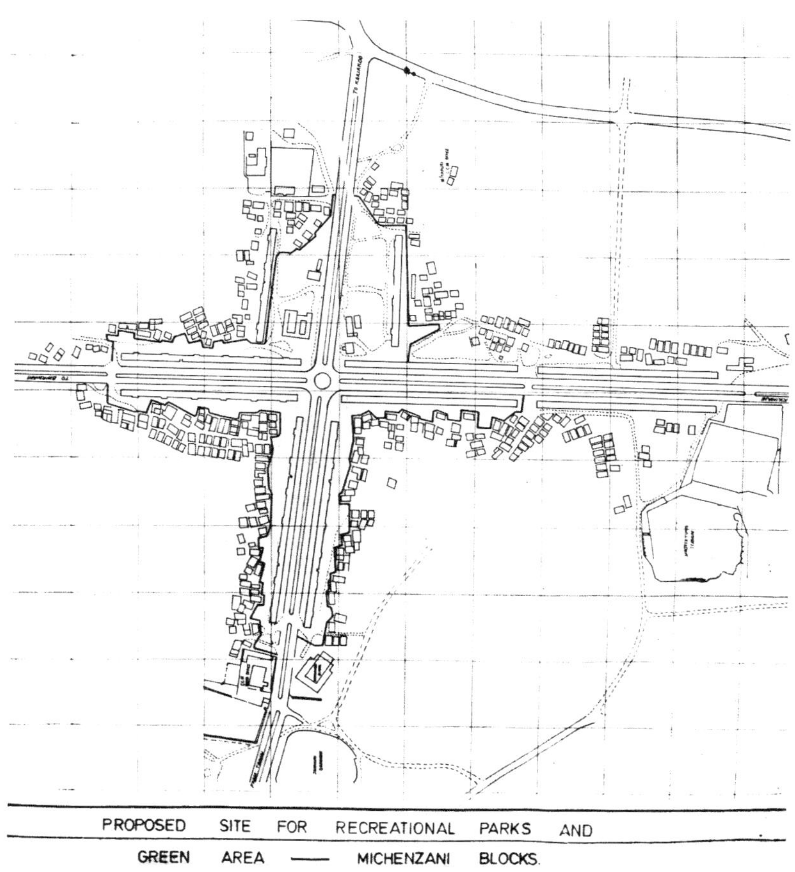

Fig 1.58: Proposed site for recreational parks and green area – Michenzani blocks (1991)

The town planner Ghalib Awadh designed a park on the scar tissue that was left after constructing the Michenzani blocks.

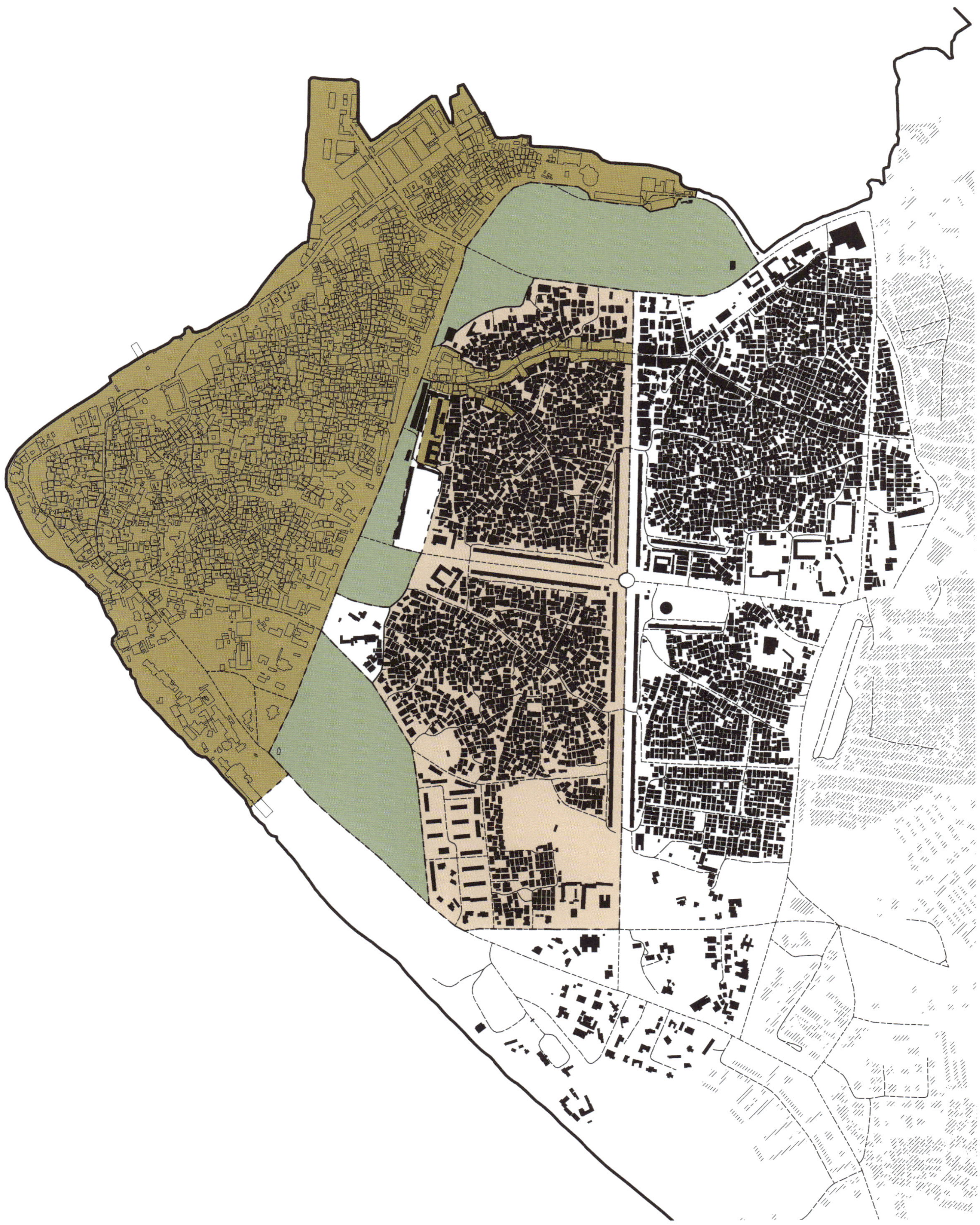

Legend

Inscribed property

Buffer zone

Buffer zone

XV. Borders of the World Heritage Site, Stone Town (1999)

Map drawn after UNESCO map showing the extent of the conservation area. The border of the WHS follows the exact outline of the racial segregation map drawn by H. V. Lanchester.

Ng'ambo, the New City Centre of Zanzibar Town (2015-2017)

Today, historic Ng'ambo with its *shehias* - including Mchangani, Vikokotoni, Mwembetanga, Kisiwandui, Kisimamajongoo, Kikwajuni Bondeni, Kikwajuni Juu, Mlandege, Gulioni, Mwembeladu, Raha Leo, Mwembeshauri, Miembeni, and parts of Kilimani, Malindi and Shangani - lies at the heart of Zanzibar Town and is earmarked as the future city centre. The pressure on this part of the city in terms of developers' interest and governmental policy is growing. There is a danger that if this is left uncontrolled, Ng'ambo may again become the object of rationalization plans leading to the replacement of the old building stock without any consideration to its historical importance and social value. Alternatively, it may become over-densified due to the encroachment on public space by private developers.

This trend applies not only to Ng'ambo, but to the whole of Zanzibar. Exponential population growth and enhanced economic activity is creating increased pressure on the scarce and environmentally fragile land of Zanzibar. In this development, the absence of planning and development regulation can be painfully felt. The masterplan for Zanzibar Town dating to 1982 aimed at a horizon of twenty years, accommodating some 200,000 inhabitants. Today the city numbers more than double that, while growth prognostics are producing staggering figures, reaching over 1,500,000 for the city alone in 2030.

The President of Zanzibar, Dr Ali Mohamed Shein, under his new government reacted to this threat by establishing an independent Department of Urban and Rural Planning (DoURP) in 2011. The DoURP, in its early existence, managed to build up a basic framework for future planning and spatial development. This commenced with the production of a *National Spatial Development Strategy*, an overarching planning vision and policy document. Alongside this, regional plans for Unguja and Pemba Islands were elaborated and the drafting of local area plans, generic policies and new planning legislation was started.

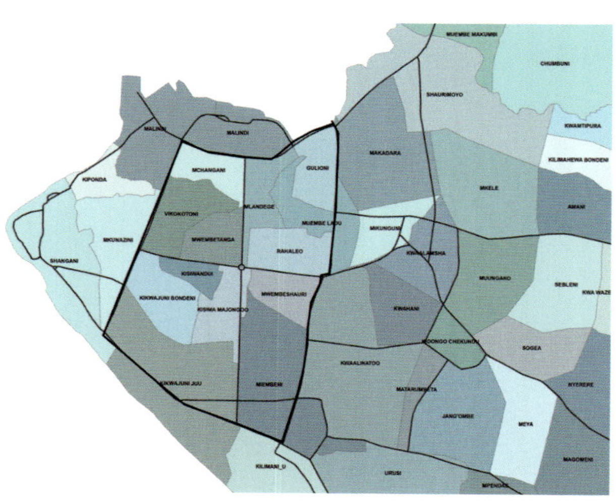

Fig 1.59: Map depicting *shehias* (2014)

The shehia *is an administrative unit which replaced the residential neighbourhoods formerly referred to as* mtaa. *The existing* shehias *have been formed by the merging of the old* mitaa. *Names of the larger* mitaa *continue to be used in the names of* shehias.

XVI. Zanzibar Town Aerial Photo (2006)

In addition, a new masterplan was commissioned from Shapira Hellerman Planners of Tel Aviv, entitled *Diagrammatic Indicative Structure Plan for Zanzibar Municipality and its Immediate Periphery and Urban Development Policy for Zanzibar Town* (ZansPlan). *ZansPlan* envisages the growth of Zanzibar Town to 1,500,000 inhabitants by 2030. It is based on three major strategic vectors: (1) to reduce sprawl and spatial coverage; (2) to retain and strengthen the current city centre as the centre of a future metropolitan system, supplemented and balanced by a set of urban centres (nodes) and radial corridors, and (3) to enable a high level of access for the city's residents based on a sustainable transport system prioritising NMT and Public Transport.

The proposed masterplan shows a radial city with three growth vectors: fingers spreading north (Bububu), east (Tunguu) and south (Fumba), with interspaced green areas. The fingers end in important sub-centres, which will give the city a polycentric configuration. The future city consists of 22 planning zones, each between 30,000 and 60,000 inhabitants. Stone Town, not dissimilar to the previous masterplans concerned with Ng'ambo, was initially excluded from the *ZansPlan*, because of its independent status and the fact that a recent update of the 1996 *Plan for the Historic Stone Town* was made in the 2008 *Stone Town Conservation Management Plan*. However, a number of planning issues concerning circulation and the Darajani area at the border with Stone Town were later included in an elaborated *City Centre Planning Zone*.

ZansPlan projects the future City Centre as a multi-use, high-density heart of the city, which needs to enhance its attractiveness to investors, tourists and residents alike. The Swahili urban tissue is left untouched but allowed to expand vertically for up to four to five floors. The main crossroads and the avenues along the northern and eastern edges are proposed to be developed as commercial high streets with a new CBD expansion suggested in Funguni. Creek Road is projected to become a central market with a public transport terminal, while the southern area is to be preserved for institutional development set in a green environment. A specific proposal concerns the artisanal market in the area called Mitiulaya, on the north-eastern border of the area included in the plan.

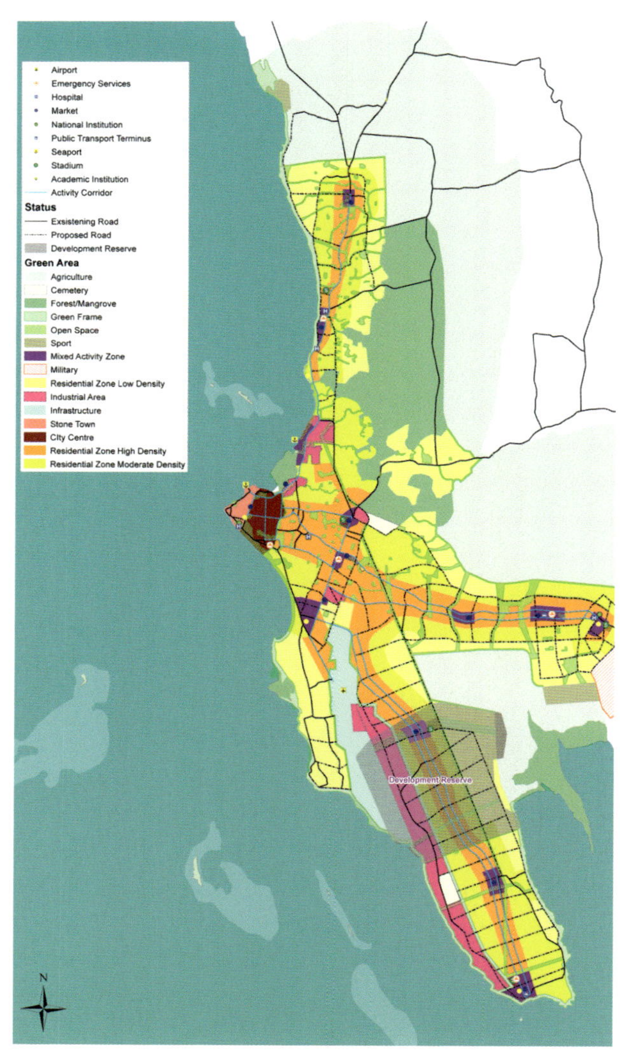

Fig 1.60: *ZansPlan* masterplan by Shapira Hellerman Planners (2015)

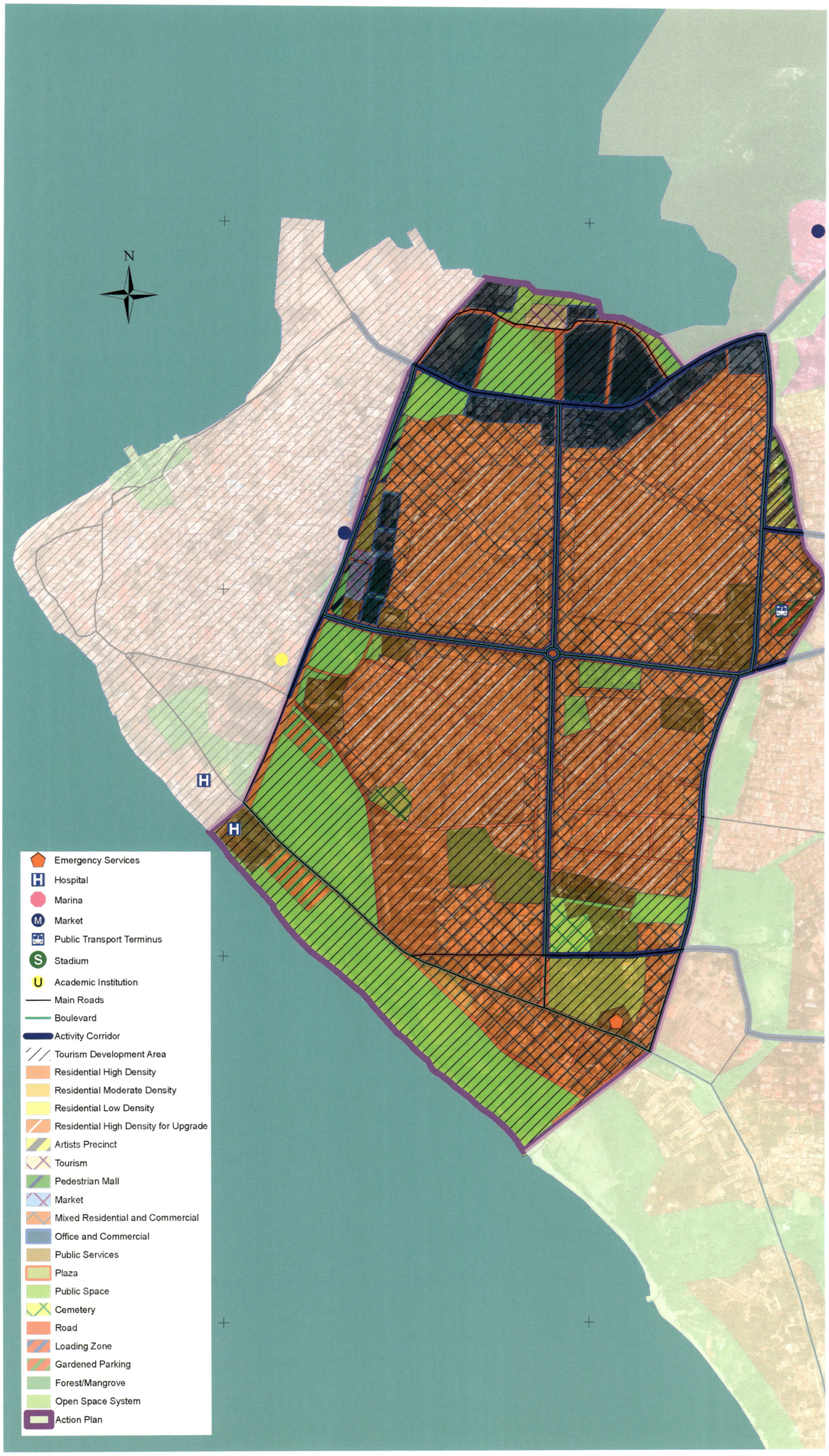

XVII. ZansPlan: City Centre Planning Zone by Shapira Hellerman Planners (2015)

The City Centre Planning Zone, situated between Stone Town and Inner City Zones, corresponds with the area covered by Ng'ambo Tuitakayo.

Ng’ambo Tuitakayo

The most recent plan for Ng’ambo is the *Zanzibar Town City Centre Local Area Plan* (hereafter referred to as LAP), which forms a part of the long-term Ng’ambo Tuitakayo research and planning project, of which this publication is one output. The project, which will be explained in more detail in Chapters 5 and 6, aims to recognize and enhance the cultural values involved in the changes in the area.

Ng’ambo Tuitakayo commenced in 2013 with a pilot research and planning project on a triangular zone formed by parts of the *shehias* of Kisiwandui, Kisimamajongoo and Michenzani. The pilot project unearthed unexpected riches in terms of cultural history, architecture, historic planning, and mapping material, which became a starting point for drafting of the LAP carried out in 2015-2016.

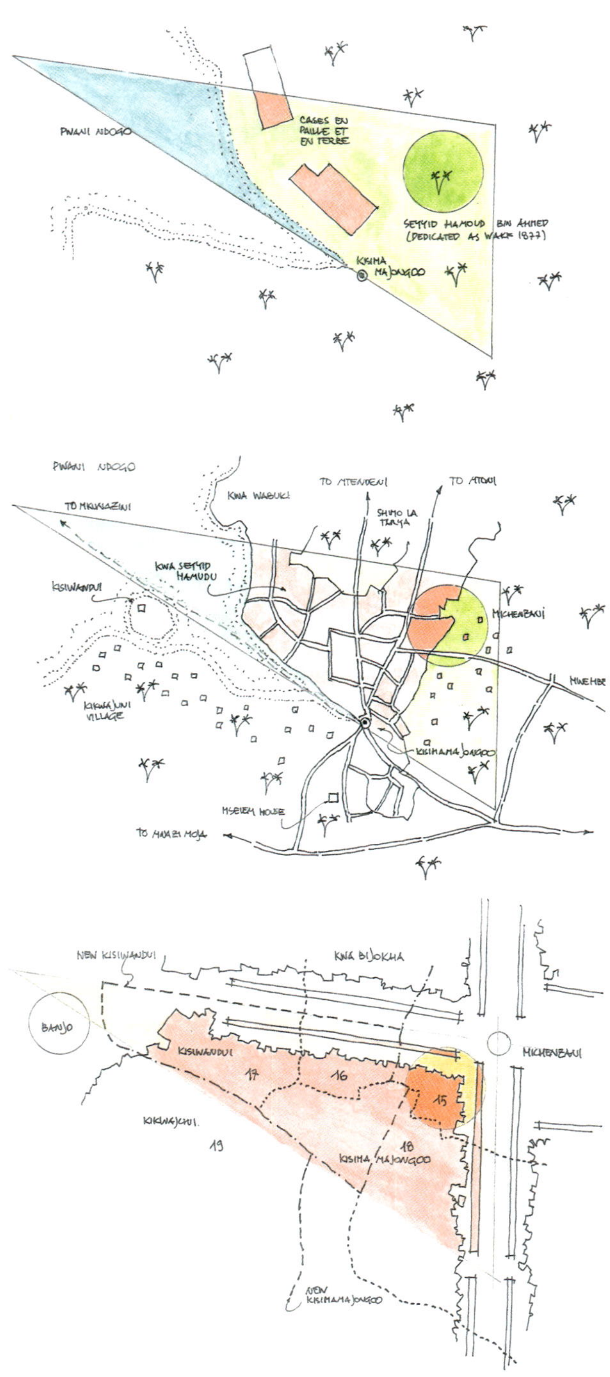

Fig 1.61: Interpretation of the development of Kisimamajongoo in three historical stages: ca.1850, ca.1960 and today

XVIII. Ng'ambo Tuitakayo: Zanzibar Town City Centre Local Area Plan (2016)

To fulfil the expectations for the new City Centre put forth in the *ZansPlan*, the following vectors of development were proposed: (1) to (re)connect people and parts of the city with its rich culture, history and natural environment; (2) to enhance the vibrancy of the City Centre through expanding commercial activity, improving public recreation facilities and culture, and (3) to protect and improve the quality of inclusive residency in the City Centre.

Today, there are viable existing nodes of activity in Ng'ambo which function independently without spatial connection. The plans set out in the LAP propose to bring together and enhance the existing nodes of activity and add new nodes of activity at strategic locations. Commerce and retail have been identified as important carriers of footfall and vibrancy heightening connectivity in the area. The existing commercial zones and markets of Darajani, Mlandege and Mapinduzi Square are to be linked through shopping streets or pedestrian malls. Recreation and tourism continue to be regarded as an important activity. The historical importance of Ng'ambo as the heart of recreation carries the potential to reassume that role by developing places like Mnazi Mmoja, Uhuru Amusement Park, Jamhuri Park and Mao Tse-Tung Stadium.

Other activities of significance which will bring people of Ng'ambo together are related to public services, such as the Mnazi Mmoja Hospital, Raha Leo Community Centre and government facilities at Mapinduzi Green Square. Mobility and public transport strategies are seen as another important creator of urban vibrancy, for which strategic nodes are to be defined, connecting Malindi Seaport, Abeid Karume International Airport and the projected sub-centres in Bububu, Fumba and Tunguu. Public transport and pedestrians will have priority over motor vehicles within the precinct of the future City Centre.

Recognising that Zanzibar Town will become a polycentric city in the future, there is a location in the plan area identified as the Central Business District (CBD). This location is at the end of the Karume Boulevard, at the junction with Felix Moumie Road and the Kariakoo Amusement Park. The location was chosen based on its central position in the network of existing and proposed facilities, including the proposed Zanzibar Metro Central Station and the new Raha Leo Community Centre, and the existing Friday Mosque and ample space available around the Central Post Office for further strategic development.

Fig 1.62: Design proposal for a housing complex in Kisimamajongoo. Master thesis by Amélie Chauvin and Alexandra Papadaki (2014)

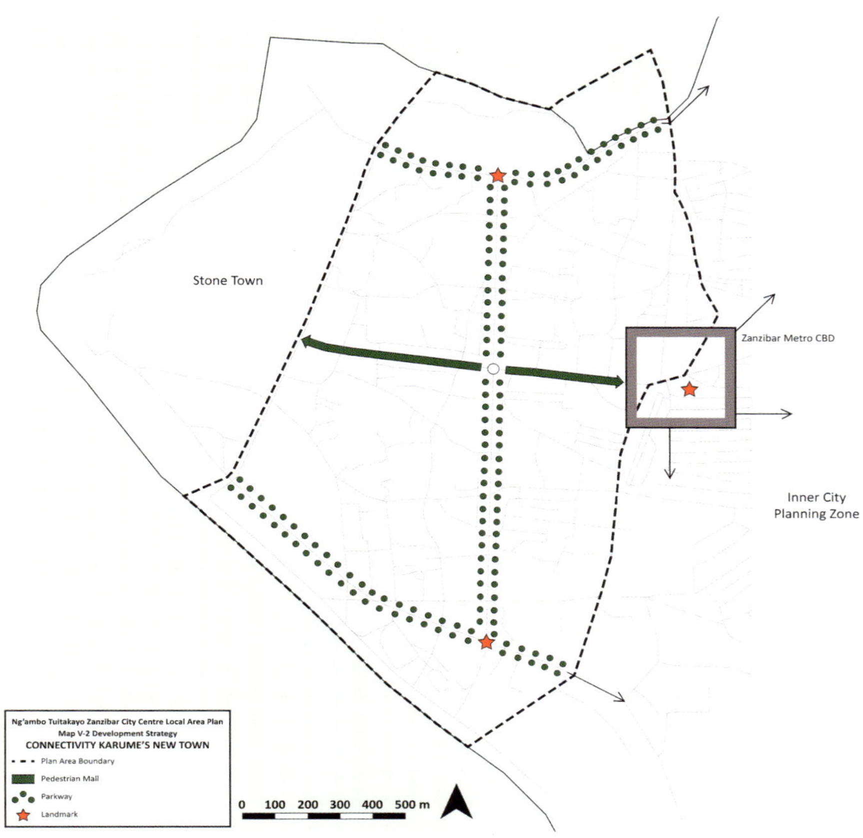

Fig 1.63: Connectivity

Map showing proposed Zanzibar Metro CBD and green corridors, from Ng'ambo Tuitakayo: Zanzibar Town City Centre Local Area Plan *(2016).*

Fig 1.64: Existing Nodes of Activity

Map showing existing nodes of activity, from Ng'ambo Tuitakayo: Zanzibar Town City Centre Local Area Plan *(2016).*

The LAP states in its strategic vision that Zanzibar Town was and is a typical Swahili city, defined by a mix of architectural and urban forms and culture. Since its beginnings it has been a cosmopolitan city which allowed a shared residency for all of its inhabitants. It was only in the 20th century that Stone Town became separated from Ng'ambo through colonial policies that frustrated the cosmopolitan nature of the city and paved the way not only for racial, but also economic segregation. In 1919, Pearce referred to Zanzibar as the 'Island Metropolis'. At that time Zanzibar Town was still the largest city in East Africa, while Zanzibar as a whole was the capital of the Swahili world and the heart of Swahili culture, stretching from Mogadishu to Sofala. Today, with its future prospects, there is no reason not to re-affirm the role of Zanzibar as a very important part of the Swahili world.

Karume, with his urban planning measures, wished to reconnect Stone Town and Ng'ambo in the most rigorous way possible, by replacing the existing city with a New Town. The LAP aims to fuse Ng'ambo with Stone Town, propelling them together into the 21st century as the City Centre of Zanzibar Town. It proposes to do this by reconnecting people and parts of the city with the rich cultural and natural environment, in a manner that respects the various layers of history manifested in the urban realm of the capital city as a whole. The resilience and inventiveness of the residents of Ng'ambo in the process of modernization of their Swahili urban culture, in spite of the neglect and the uprooting of their environment through the New Town project, is a key to the proposed integral development of residency in Zanzibar Town City Centre. The aim is to develop a modern city for all.

Fig 1.65: Design proposal for gardens providing shade south of Mapembeani open space and design proposal for school building and Mapembeani open space by Mia Callenberg (2016)

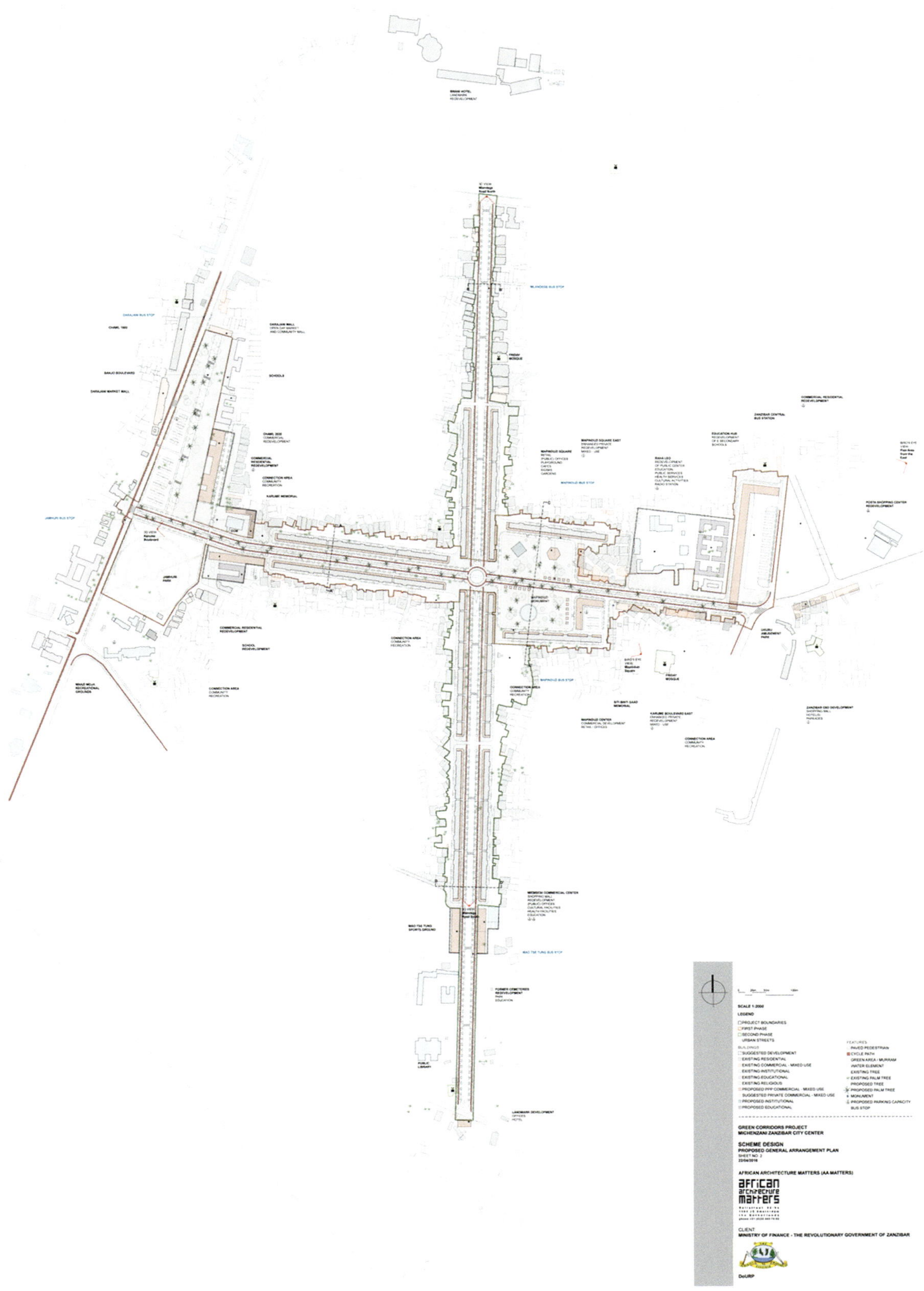

Fig 1.66: Michenzani green corridors plan (2016)

City Centre ideas were further developed into the Michenzani Green Corridors development scheme in 2016. This detailed scheme draws on the principles and visions outlined in ZansPlan *and the* Zanzibar Town City Centre Local Area Plan. *It proposes broad pedestrian walkways with new commercial, cultural and educational facilities. In addition, it proposes an overall greening of the public space of the existing Mlandege Rd. and Karume Boulevard, linking Stone Town to the planned Zanzibar Metro CBD with a public transport terminal and high-rise commercial, recreational and residential buildings.*

2

Cultural Landscape of Ng'ambo

Ng'ambo's cultural landscape consists of many tangible and intangible layers, of which only a small fraction is included on the following pages. The material presented in this chapter was collected through field surveys and provides records of the existing (physical) situation as well as visible, semi-visible and invisible traces of history, traditions and customs shaping the urban realm of Zanzibar Town. The investigated topics are presented as separate categories for practical reasons, but it is useful to remember, while considering them separately, that in reality they always manifest together.

Urban Typologies

Urban typologies were defined based on the following criteria: density of building development, degree of formality, function and/or prevailing historical characteristics.

Explanation of terms

Bazaar Street: commercial areas developed along narrow streets, traditionally lined with rows of Indian shopfront buildings.

Grid Swahili Urban: planned or semi-planned urban areas developed on an orthogonal grid pattern, historically comprising single-storey Swahili buildings.

High Street: emerging business and commerce areas such as the northern part of Mlandege Road and parts of Malawi Road. Characterized by multi-storey buildings of mixed use with retail and service located predominantly on the ground floors. Term borrowed from the urban phenomenon typically found in the United Kingdom.

Institutional Complex: areas characterized by a high number of institutional buildings.

Karume New Town: urban areas developed as a part of President Karume's rehabilitation project for Ng'ambo in the 1960s and 1970s. Typically characterized by modernist architecture.

Low Density: urban areas of predominantly residential character, and with relatively broad streets, located on the edges of the city and characterized predominantly by detached family houses surrounded by gardens.

Organic Swahili Urban: urban areas that have developed organically over years. The existing pattern of streets, open and built-up areas has not been predefined, but has taken form gradually, influenced to a large degree by its inhabitants. Historically the areas are dominated by single-storey Swahili buildings.

Temporary Commercial Area: makeshift commercial areas developed organically over time.

Legend

- Bazaar Street
- Grid Swahili Urban
- High Street
- Institutional Complex
- Karume New Town
- Low Density
- Organic Swahili Urban
- Temporary Commercial Area

XIX. Urban Typologies

XIX. Urban Typologies

Building Typology

Buildings in the area were classified according to their current primary use. As a result of limited capacity, aspects such as ground surface and floor surface were not taken into account when surveying the buildings, and were not considered while defining the individual typologies. Among the surveyed buildings, buildings identified as residential constitute the largest category in the area. The category was further divided into seven sub-categories. The residential sub-categories identified include buildings with no typological forerunners in the area and buildings which can be considered as variations of building types traditional to the area.

One of the main factors serving to differentiate between the typologies within the category of residential buildings was the relation of the building to the street and to the footprint of the single-storey Swahili house. While it has not been subject to a detailed investigation, there is a suspicion that typologies such as the multi-storey Swahili and Swahili 2020 repeat in their floorplans a layout modelled on the floorplan of the single-storey Swahili house. Other buildings found in the area were grouped under the following categories: commercial, public and government, educational and religious (for more detailed information on each of the categories see below and glossary).

In total, 4,694 buildings in the area were attributed a building typology. The number of buildings with no typology attributed (indicating buildings under construction or in ruins) is 161 (3.4%). These buildings have not been included in the table. Residential buildings constitute 87 percent of the surveyed building stock, of which the single-storey Swahili house is the prevailing type, representing 77 percent of all residential units.

From the survey it also emerges that multi-storey Swahili and Swahili 2020 buildings, considered as typological continuations of the single-storey Swahili houses, are usually found integrated into the single-storey Swahili tissue located, primarily, on roads or at crossroads accessible by car. The largest number of Swahili 2020 buildings in proportion to the overall number of buildings can be found in the north-eastern and south-western areas. The survey also indicates a comparatively high percentage of apartment buildings (2.5%) and suburban villas (2.2%). While the high percentage of the former can be attributed to the modernist building stock present in the area, the latter category was applied to all detached family houses in the area that have little or no interaction with street activities.

The survey indicates that government buildings make up a very small percentage of area's total building stock (0.9%). It also emerges from the map that they are usually located along the main roads. The greatest diversity of building typologies is found on the northern edges of the area, in Mchangani and Mlandege, and in particular along Mlandege Road, where the concentration of the high-street typology (0.6%), itself a recent contribution to the urban landscape of Ng'ambo, is the highest. Market stalls represent a relatively high percentage of the total building stock (5.6%), and their largest concentration can be found in Kwa Haji Tumbo and in Raha Leo. The percentage of buildings hosting educational institutions is 1.6 percent (madrasas, private and public schools). There are 28 mosques in Ng'ambo, which are distributed across the four quarters in proportion to the overall number of structures in each quarter. The category 'others', which describes service, hospitality, utility, public and non-conforming residential buildings, was assigned to 71 buildings. Buildings categorized as others are usually found at the edges of the otherwise densely built single-storey Swahili tissue.

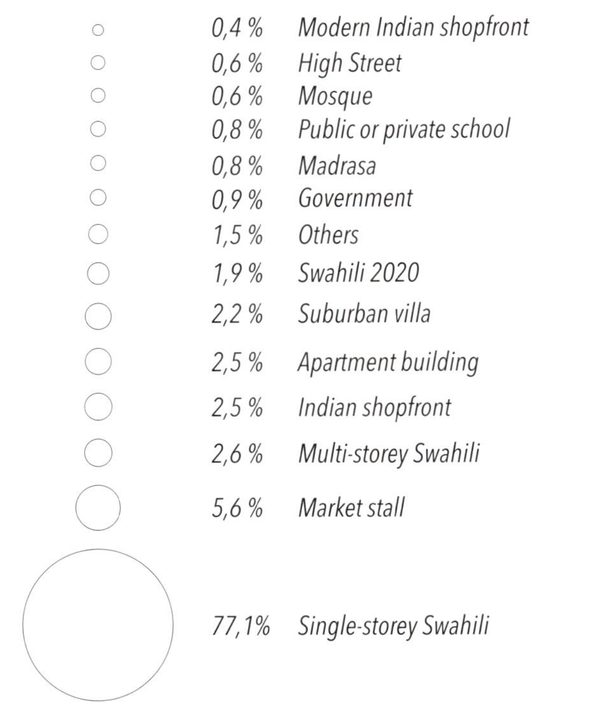

Building Typology

Legend

- Single-storey Swahili
- Multi-storey Swahili
- Swahili 2020
- Apartment building
- Suburban villa
- Market stall
- Indian shopfront
- Modern Indian shopfront
- High Street
- Public or private school
- Madrasa
- Mosque
- Government
- Others
- In ruins
- Under construction
- Information missing

XX. Building Typology

XX. Building Typology

Residential buildings

Residential buildings make up the largest number in the existing building stock. There are several typologies that can be identified within this category, but the single-storey Swahili house is the most common. Despite formal changes occurring over time (as a result of improvements and alterations of the buildings, or new trends present in the area) the structures largely follow their local prototype. This is customarily characterized by a rectangular, one-storey house with three to six rooms arranged around an axial corridor, with outbuildings comprising kitchen and toilet located at the back and separated by a small courtyard from the living area.

The decorative treatment of the outer walls in the single-storey Swahili houses is traditionally minimal, with a more elaborate detailing given to the front elevation. Here, as in Stone Town one will find carved doors and frames, which customarily indicate the wealth and status of the people living behind them. The typology also marks a transition from public to private space by means of a *baraza*: a stone bench located either on both sides of the entrance, or within a deep recess beside it. Formal alterations of single-storey Swahili houses occur most frequently on the exterior, leaving the internal layout largely unaltered. The most common alterations include the addition of burglar guards and door gates (often fashioned with wrought iron), the addition of a portico with columns; high gables, crenulations, balustrades, or, for instance, the re-location of the entrance from the front of the building to the side on which a portico has been newly added.

Single-storey Swahili houses were traditionally built with wattle and daub, a building material no longer used in new constructions. Upgrading and modernization of residential buildings is primarily achieved through changes in building materials and technology, employing more permanent materials such as concrete frames or cement blocks, and through vertical extension. However, upgrading can also take form of aesthetic improvements to the exterior of the building. These are often regarded as a manifestation of the owner's affluence. Two types of residential buildings – the multi-storey Swahili and the Swahili 2020 – are built on the same footprint as the single-storey Swahili house, but have more than one storey and are, in general, more recent additions to the streetscapes of the area. Other important residential typologies are apartment buildings and suburban villas. Both typologies are constructed with little regard to the wider context of the street.

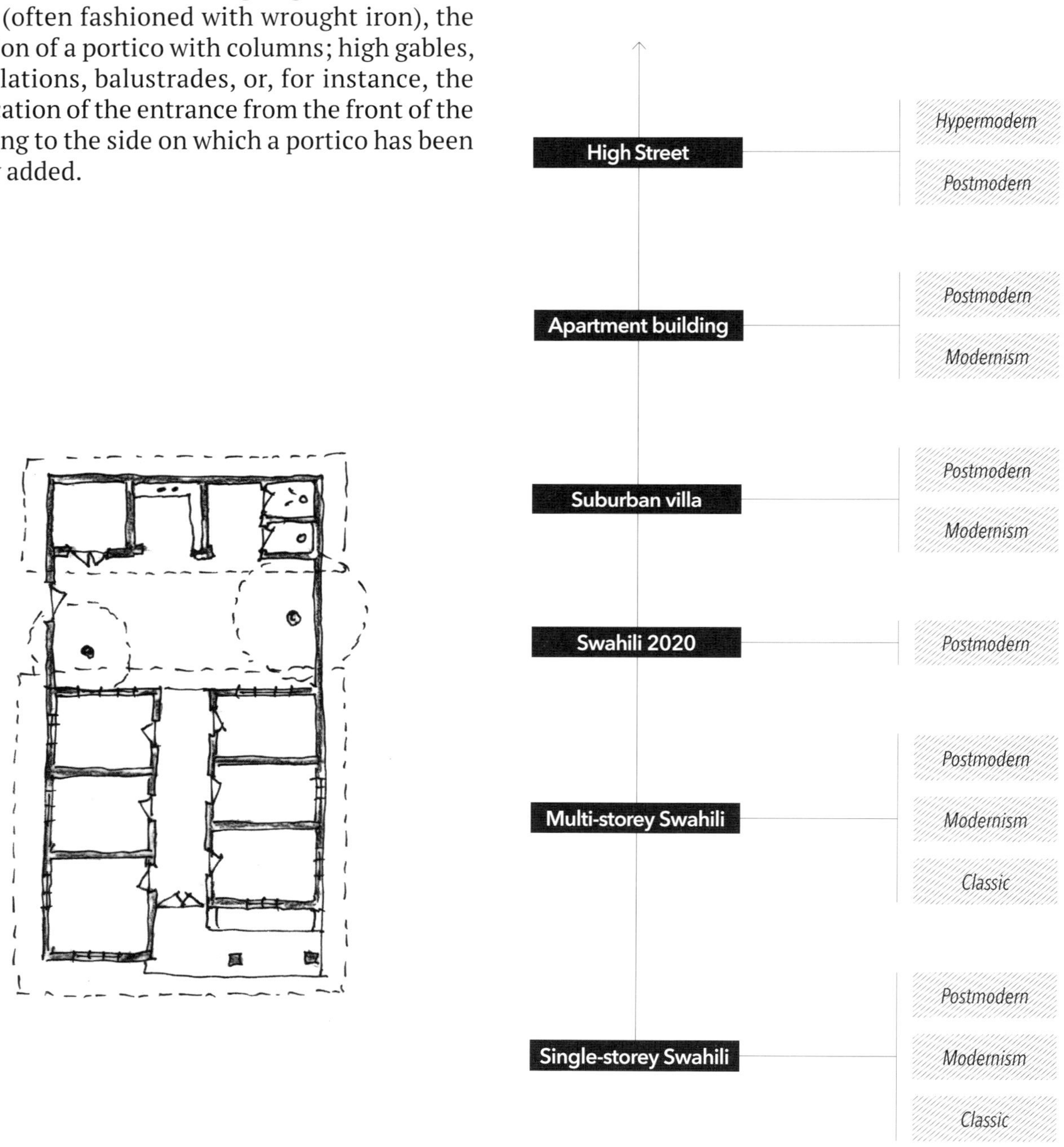

Fig 2.1: Floor-plan of a single-storey Swahili house and genealogy of residential typologies

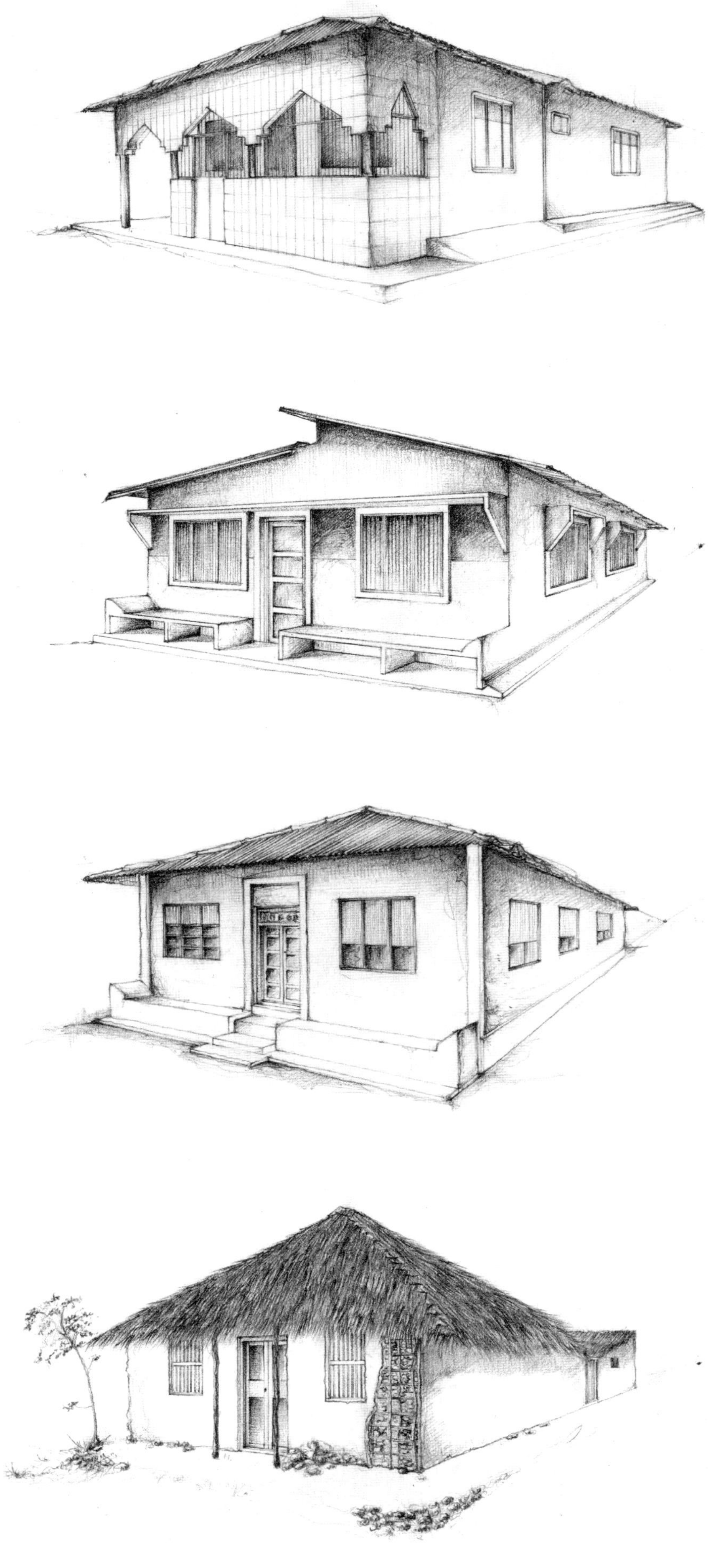

Fig 2.2: Single-storey Swahili: building styles – classic, modernism and postmodern

Commercial buildings

Commercial activity is fundamental to both the built environment and social fabric of the Swahili neighbourhood, making it rather difficult to discern a strictly commercial type of building in the area. General stores and grocery shops, or *dukas*, are usually located on the ground floors of buildings or in parts of the single-storey Swahili houses. Among the typologies combining residential and commercial functions, the Indian shopfront is particularly notable for its distinctive architecture. Indian shopfronts are usually built in rows and have commercial activity – spanning everything from grocery and wholesale to hardware and carpentry – located on the ground floor with living quarters above them. Many of the retail buildings along the narrow streets of Ng'ambo are in fact variations of the Indian shopfront buildings. Otherwise, one of the most widespread purpose-built commercial structures is the market stall. Market stalls come in many different forms, but are usually characterized by makeshift materials and are either free-standing or built adjacent to houses. In recent years, the area has also experienced a rapid growth of the service sector translated into the emergence of a new mixed-use building type – the high-street building.

Fig 2.3: View of a *duka*

Public and government buildings

Public and government buildings have traditionally been located in Stone Town, hence their overall number in Ng'ambo is relatively low. While this disproportion can primarily be attributed to the colonial period, not much effort has been put into providing the area with new public and government buildings since the revolution. Karume's efforts focused primarily on large-scale residential developments, and his government usually appropriated old colonial buildings for its own institutions. Among the purpose-built government buildings from Karume's time are the former ASP headquarters in Vikokotoni (today CCM Headquarters) and the building of the Department of Public Works by the Michenzani Roundabout (once functioning as the Zanzibar New Town building office). Today, the government offices in Ng'ambo, apart from a couple of newly erected buildings, are scattered around the area, often located in former colonial buildings or more substantial residences adapted for new use.

Fig 2.4: Ministry of Foreign Affairs and International Cooperation

Over the years, there has been only one post office servicing Ng'ambo from within the boundaries of the surveyed area. The office was located in Raha Leo and is currently no longer in use. Today, the nearest post office is in Kijangwani beyond Felix Moumie Road. The overall number of public health services has remained unchanged since colonial times and includes the Mnazi Mmoja Hospital, Maternity Hospital and the Raha Leo Dispensary. A notable and relatively recent addition to the stock of public buildings in Ng'ambo is the Public Library in Miembeni.

Educational buildings

There are three major types of educational institution in Ng'ambo: public schools, private schools and madrasas. Public schools are predominantly one or two-storey structures built around an inner courtyard. Most of the schools were constructed during the British Protectorate.

Fig 2.5: A school in Kisiwandui

The schools located along Creek Road were designed in a distinctive British colonial style and can be considered as the 'urban type of school', which is stylistically more elaborate and more compact in its layout than schools found in rural areas. The first school built in Ng'ambo was the Ng'ambo School for Girls in Raha Leo, which opened in 1943. Another important (though no longer existing) educational facility was the Gulioni Trade School located at the current location of the Bank of Tanzania. Private schools and madrasas can often be found in older buildings adapted for new use, or in structures adjoining residential units and mosques. Some of the newer madrasas and private schools are located in purpose-built, multi-storey structures.

Religious buildings

Ng'ambo is home to various religious communities, however none of the places of worship apart from mosques have a visible impact on its contemporary urban landscape. The architecture of mosques varies depending on their time of construction. Many of the structures found in the area remain in their original locations (*see* Chapter 1, p. 30). Some of the mosques are housed in inconspicuous structures, whereas the appearance of others has been altered over the years often to become more elaborate than their predecessors. The strategic importance of mosques in community life determines their central location within the urban fabric. Older mosques will usually be found within the densely built tissue. Newer, larger and more imposing in their appearance, Friday mosques built during the past three decades can be found in Mwembeshauri, Mlandege and Gulioni.

Fig 2.6: Biziredi Mosque

Building Styles

The area comprises predominantly self-built houses. It would therefore be counterproductive to look for coherent stylistic expressions in the common understanding of that word. Instead, the decision was made to consider the style of a building not so much as an essential category, but as a tool indicating common characteristics found in the external appearance of the structures. This approach has enabled insights into the transformations taking place in the area. Building styles that were identified can be considered as reflections of various vernacular trends, individual, communal and governmental aspirations and, in some instances, indications of a specific historical period. Because of their broad application, building styles should be considered in relation to the typology that they are describing (for more detailed information on each of the styles see the glossary).

The stylistic categories that were identified do not account for all the varieties of architectural expression present in the area. Sometimes, the transformations could not be captured in terms of stylistic description, while in other cases buildings were simply devoid of distinctive elements that would permit identifying them with a particular style. In these cases the buildings were either left without a style or assigned one of the existing styles based on the subjective judgement of the surveyor.

Among the single-storey Swahili buildings, the largest number of buildings were attributed the Classic Swahili style (82 percent of the single-storey Swahili buildings that were surveyed). The map also indicates a considerably large number of buildings that were given the postmodern style. It should be noted that the respective styles do not indicate the moment of the initial construction of the building since the decorative elements on the exterior of the building are usually applied irrespective of structural changes within the building. Based on the findings made during the research it can also be concluded that the set of decorative elements associated with modernist and postmodern styles can be related to a certain period in time and reflect the prevailing (decorative) trend of the moment.

For the remaining typologies there is a relatively high percentage of buildings attributed the postmodern style, of which a particularly high concentration can be found in Mwembeladu and Mlandege. The map also shows that buildings in a postmodern style (irrespective of their typology) will often be located close to each other. Although it is difficult to distinguish a clear pattern, it appears that when making changes to the appearance of their buildings, owners are often influenced by the decoration found in neighbouring houses. Modernism is another well-represented style (7.9%). This is partially due to the extensive modernist interventions of the 1960s and 1970s, but the style can also be found in other residential and public buildings from the 1940s, 50s, and 60s. The area has a high percentage of buildings without a designated style (12.7%), including market stalls and functional buildings often not conforming to any of the established categories. The presence of the remaining styles in the area is marginal, apart from the Indian-influenced style, in the form of the Indian shopfront typology found along Darajani Street.

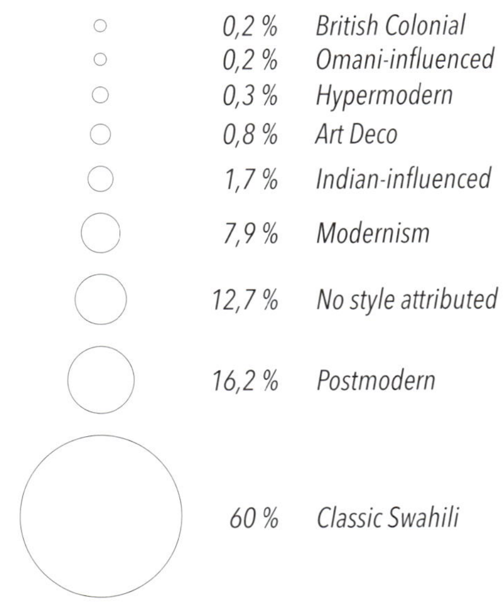

Building Styles

Legend

SINGLE-STOREY SWAHILI
- Classic Swahili
- Art Deco
- Modernism
- Postmodern

OTHER TYPOLOGIES
- Indian-influenced
- Omani-influenced
- British Colonial
- Art Deco
- Modernism
- Postmodern
- Hypermodern
- No style attributed
- In ruins
- Information missing

XXI. Building Styles

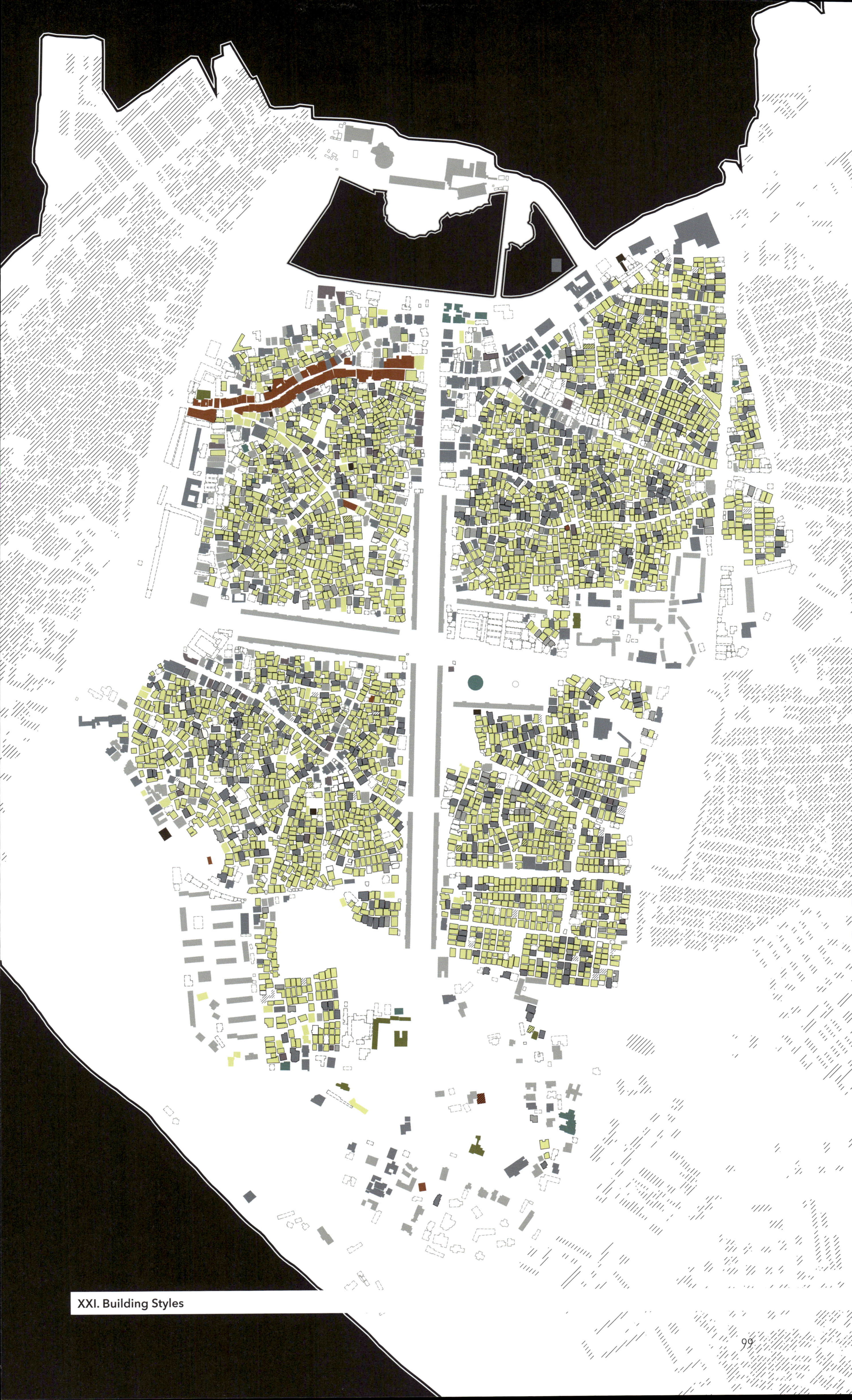

XXI. Building Styles

Fig 2.7: Classic Swahili

Fig 2.8: Postmodern

Fig 2.9: Postmodern

Fig 2.10: Modernism

Fig 2.11: Suburban villa

Fig 2.12: Suburban villa

Fig 2.13: Swahili 2020

Fig 2.14: Under construction

Fig 2.15: Art Deco

Fig 2.16: Hypermodern

Fig 2.17: Others

Fig 2.18: Multi-storey Swahili

Fig 2.19: Others

Fig 2.20: Apartment building

Fig 2.21: Postmodern

Fig 2.22: Commercial building (Modern Indian shopfront)

Building Condition

The survey included an external assessment of the condition of all the buildings within the boundaries of the area. The assessment was carried out based on the structural condition, cosmetic appearance and the grade of maintenance of the individual structures. Where possible, all four sides of the buildings were examined, in other cases the main façade and side elevations were used as indicators of the overall condition of the building. Given the skin-deep nature of the undertaken assessment, it is likely that the actual condition of individual buildings in the area is worse than indicated by the survey.

Buildings were assessed according to the following five categories:

Good: building appears structurally sound and shows evidence of regular maintenance.

Average: building doesn't have visible structural defects, but shows signs of wear and tear and recent repairs, possibly missing exterior plaster, with exposed cement blocks and or/coral stone and damage to the roof structure.

Poor: building shows advanced stages of deterioration and may have serious structural problems. There are no signs of maintenance work.

Under construction: the building is under construction.

In ruins: building is either partially or totally collapsed.

The results of the survey show that the majority of buildings in the area are of average condition. Nearly one-fifth of the assessed buildings are in poor condition, while 14 percent of the total building stock is considered to be in good condition. When broken down according to location, the numbers show that the concentration of buildings in poor condition is higher in the parts of town which are located further away from Stone Town, such as Gulioni, Mwembeladu or Kisimamajongoo. Correspondingly, the areas with the fewest poorly maintained buildings and the highest number of buildings in good condition are Vikokotoni, Mchangani and Mwembetanga, all of which are located nearby the Darajani Market.

It also emerges from the map that buildings of good and poor condition are generally arranged in clusters of two or more, and will less often be found in isolated locations. The map also indicates a relatively high percentage of buildings under construction. This could be considered as an indication of the building activity taking place in the area. However, it should also be noted that some of the buildings remain in a perpetual state of construction, which makes it impossible to judge whether they will ever be completed or if they will eventually turn into ruins.
Information gathered during the research suggests that there is a general tendency among residents to consider postmodern style as a form of improvement and modernization of a building. Observations made in the field also suggest that, in general, observers are more likely to deem the condition of a single-storey Swahili house in a postmodern style as good than that of a Classic Swahili.

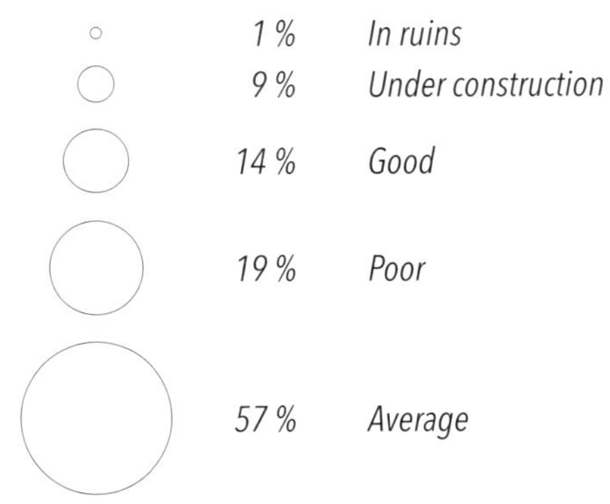

Building Condition

Legend

Good

Average

Poor

In ruins

Under construction

Information missing

XXII. Building Condition

XXII. Building Condition

Building Technology: Walls and Structural Frame

Five distinct types of building technology were identified, representing both traditional building technologies and building technologies introduced to the area in the second half of the 20th century. Historically, buildings in Ng'ambo were wattle and daub and coral stone structures, while the use of cement blocks first became widespread after the revolution, and continues to be the dominant building material in one- and two-storey buildings today (64.3%). As can be seen on the map, the overall distribution of the respective building technologies across the area is quite even. However, the total percentage of the respective building technologies varies within the respective areas depending on the typologies found in each of them.

The percentage of concrete-frame and cement-block structures in the area is relatively low, making up only 10.7 percent of the total building stock. This can generally be attributed to the low-rise character of the Zanzibar Town at large. While steadily growing, the number of buildings higher than two storeys is still relatively small in Ng'ambo. This explains the low percentage of buildings employing concrete frames in their structures, as this is a building technology usually reserved for contemporary developments of more than two storeys. The largest concentration of buildings using concrete frame and cement blocks is therefore found in commercial areas currently undergoing rapid development, such as Mlandege Road and Darajani Street.

At the time of the survey there were only six buildings constructed using wattle and daub remaining in the area (one building respectively in Kikwajuni Bondeni, Kikwajuni Juu, Miembeni, Mwembeshauri, Mwembeladu and Mlandege). While wattle and daub is no longer in use as a building material in the area, rubble masonry will still be found in secondary structures such as boundary walls and shacks. In addition, the map identifies structures made of makeshift materials. These make up less than 2 percent of the total building stock and usually pertain to market stalls or temporary structures scattered around the area.

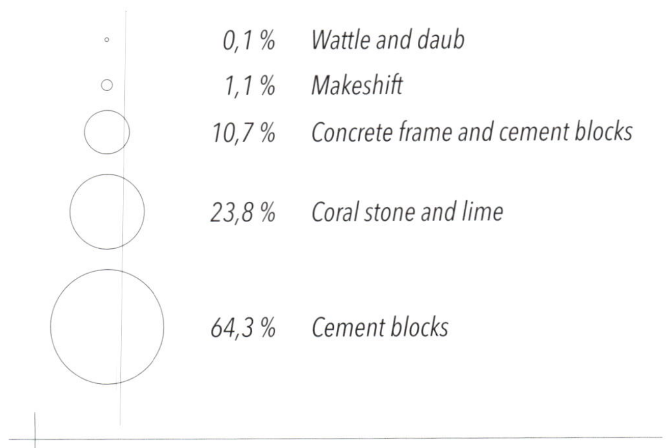

Building Technology: Walls and Structural Frame

Legend

- Cement blocks
- Concrete frame and cement blocks
- Coral stone and lime
- Wattle and daub
- Makeshift
- In ruins
- Under construction
- Information missing

XXIII. Building Technology: Walls and Structural Frame

XXIII. Building Technology: Walls and Structural Frame

Building Technology: Roof Structure and Outer Layer

The survey included an external assessment of roof structures and covers. Buildings were grouped according to four categories, of which the timber frame covered with metal sheets was the dominant one in the area. The large percentage of buildings employing this structure indicates that its use is not only restricted to single-storey Swahili houses, but is also applied in other typologies. The widespread use of the timber frame and metal sheets can be attributed to the affordability and accessibility of these materials, whereas the relatively high percentage of concrete-slab roofs (5.9%) indicates a growing tendency to use concrete slabs in contemporary, mostly high-street, developments. This also applies to the modernist architecture present in Ng'ambo. The highest concentration of buildings with concrete-slab roofs can be found in the area of Mlandege Road, one of the areas with the highest number of recent developments. Bush-pole frame and *makuti* roofs, which were historically the first roof covers used in the area, have nearly vanished from Ng'ambo. There are no new residential units employing this type of cover and it is a matter of time before the *makuti* roofs of the few remaining single-storey Swahili houses are replaced with metal-sheets. Nevertheless, it seems that the *makuti* roof is not set to disappear entirely from the urban landscape of Ng'ambo as it continues to be used on smaller structures providing public entertainment and places for socializing such as local restaurants, *maskani*, market stalls or *dukas*, marking their distinct function in the otherwise predominantly residential neighbourhoods.

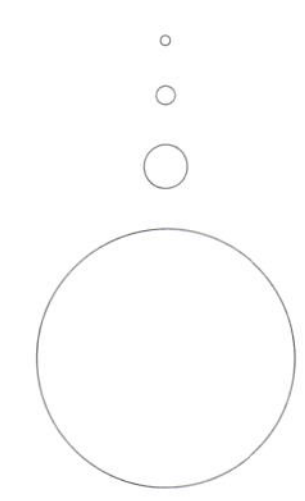

Building Technology: Roof Structure and Outer Layer

Legend

- Timber frame and metal sheets
- Timber frame and roof tiles
- Concrete slab
- Bush-pole frame and *makuti* thatching
- In ruins
- Under construction
- Information missing

XXIV. Building Technology: Roof Structure and Outer Layer

XXIV. Building Technology: Roof Structure and Outer Layer

Building Heights

Legend

1 storey

2 storeys

3 storeys

4 storeys

5 storeys

6 storeys

7 storeys

8 storeys

9 storeys

In ruins

Under construction

Information missing

XXV. Building Heights

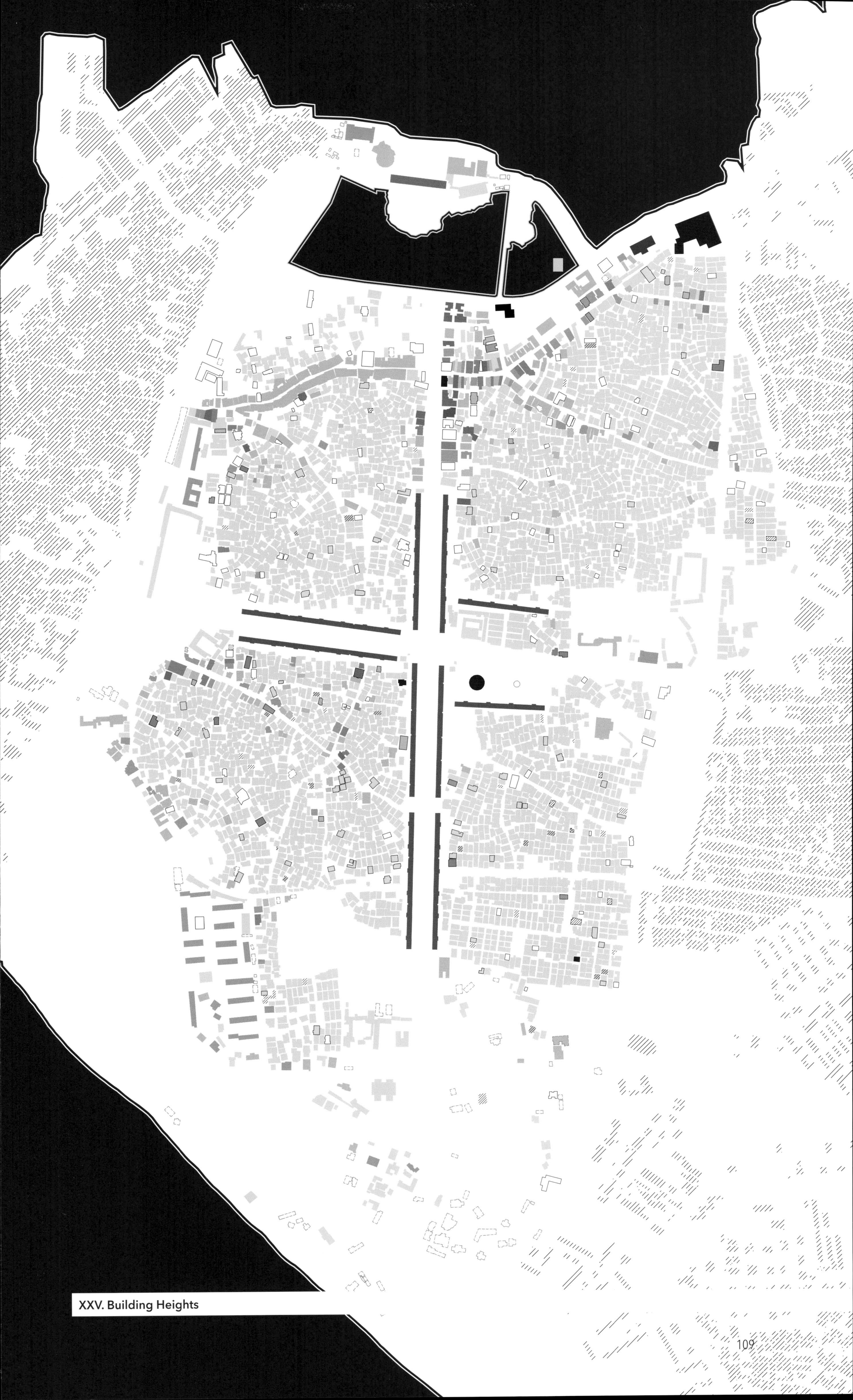

XXV. Building Heights

Toponymy

Place names found in Ng'ambo's neighbourhoods reveal many details of area's history. The majority of names indicated on the map are historical names which have been in constant use by the community for over a hundred years. They provide clues to the thoughts, lives and customs of Ng'ambo's residents and are important elements of people's collective memory.[27] The origins of names occurring in the area are various, but unlike many other Swahili cities subjected to colonial rule, they have maintained their indigenous roots. As noted by Myers, most of the place names in Ng'ambo are given by people based on the everyday, customary world around them: trees, activities, land-ownership, well-known personalities, or natural features.[28] Many of the stories behind the names are still known by the people, but there are also names whose roots are unknown, or which elicit varied, sometimes conflicting stories.

A comparison of names on old maps with those present in the area today shows that despite changing geographical references, the majority of historical names have stood the test of time and continue to figure prominently in inhabitants' mental map of the city. But there are names, such as the ones referring to landowners or *wakf* trustees – Kwa Hema ('at Hema') referring to Remtulla bin Hema, an Asian businessman and plantation owner, or Seyid Hamudu, a *wakf* trustee – which have fallen from use (*see* Chapter 1, Map V). The only name indicating landownership mentioned by the inhabitants during the mapping was that of the female plantation owner Biziredi.

The toponymy of Ng'ambo's urban landscape is dynamic and multi-layered and describes various aspects of area's urban texture. The more contemporary names and nicknames given to places for social gatherings are beyond the scope of this study, but it does not make them any less relevant for the understanding of city's cultural landscape. In contrast to the Swahili historical names, they often derive from English and refer to places outside of Zanzibar. *Maskani*, popular meeting places for men, can be given names, depending on their character, such as Brooklyn, Ajax Amsterdam and Sao Paolo Madrid, or others alluding to difficult and rough lifestyles such as Taffran Time ('tough times'), Bad Boys and More Trick, with their names often figuring prominently on the walls.[29]

[27] Garth Andrew Myers, "Naming and Placing the Other: Power and Urban Landscape in Zanzibar", in *Critical Toponymies: The Contested Politics of Place Naming*, eds. Lawrence D. Berg and Jani Vuolteenaho (London, Routledge, 2009), pp. 85-100.

[28] Ibid., p. 91.

[29] More on the *maskan* phenomenon in Zanzibar can be found in Mohammed Ali Bakari, *The Democratisation Process in Zanzibar: A Retarded Transition* (Hamburg, Insitut für Afrika-Kunde, 2001), pp. 179-95.

"Many street names disappeared when the Michenzani blocks were built. Now they are just called Michenzani. But there were many different names, like the 64 Street, which I don't know the meaning of actually, but other names were mostly related to the names of bands that used to play here in this neighbourhood. There were many! The Islanders, the band I played for, Stardust, Cosmopolitan, Zanzibar Jazz band. There was also a place called Ngazi Nje, which referred to the house with the outdoor stairs. But with the building of the blocks, all these places and hence their names disappeared."

Idi Ali Abubaka, born in 1944 in Kisiwandui, lives in a flat in Michenzani blocks.

The *maskan* Bad Boys is located alongside the Michenzani block in Kisiwandui and has been a gathering place mostly for young men for over thirty years. If asked why the *maskan* was called Bad Boys, men would commonly answer, 'just because'. An older man explained it was kind of a joke: *"They are not bad boys, look at them, but if people think they are, people can think that, we know better."* Another man who normally lives in Dar es Salaam, but returned to Zanzibar for the celebration of Ramadan, when asked about the importance of the *maskan*, said:

"Yes of course [it is important to us], this is what we have inherited from our parents and that we will pass on to the next generations." He pointed at other, younger men: *"Because this is our culture, this is what we do. We talk with each other, we share ideas, we support each other, this is our culture. And this is what I miss in Dar es Salaam. This is really something we will miss if it is gone. And 'this' is not just a* maskan, *this is home."*

Images 2.23-2.25:

In contrast to the baraza, *which is a traditional element of Swahili houses,* maskani *first became a prominent feature of Zanzibar's urban landscape in the 1990s.*

Fig 2.23: More Trick *maskan*

Fig 2.24: Cowboy Sound System *maskan*

Fig 2.25: Sao Paulo Madrid *maskan*

Names in the map come into the following categories: trees, natural features, cultural-historical, everyday economic activities, and people-related. Selected examples from each category have been described briefly below.

Trees

Trees play an important role in the life of the local community, especially the mango trees. They are valued for their healing and spiritual properties. They have economic value and provide shade from the bright sun, making them perfect locations for various community activities. Interestingly enough, the majority of trees referred to in Ng'ambo's place names are not endemic to the tropical biome of Zanzibar, but have been brought in by the European, Indian, or Arab traders passing through the island over the centuries. In Ng'ambo, over 30 percent of *mitaa* are named after trees, testifying to their importance for the area. These include, among others: Miembeni ('at the mango trees'), Mbuyuni ('at the baobab tree'), Mnazi Mmoja ('the single coconut tree'), Mtendeni ('at the date tree'), and so forth.

Natural features

Many of the names in the area are derived from features characteristic to the given place. For instance, the road separating Stone Town from Ng'ambo is known by the name Creek Road, referring to the tidal creek which was once there. The creek was crossed by a bridge, which today lends its name to one of the main shopping streets in the area, Darajani Street ('at the bridge'). The *mtaa* Kisimamajongoo, 'the well overrun by millipedes', is named after the well that was probably situated on the high ground at the major crossing in the area, at the beginning of a small stream that fed into the creek (*see* Chapter 1, Map V). The name of the *mtaa* Vikokotoni indicates 'the area of small pebbles', Mchangani is 'the sandy area along the creek', while Mayungwani indicates a type of plant that used to grow in the area.

Cultural-historical

Names of trees are often paired with cultural or social activities taking place in their shade. The tree featuring most frequently in names across the area is *mwembe*, the mango tree. One would go for advice to Mwembeshauri, dance *ngoma rikunda* (traditional dance) at Mwemberikunda and play the traditional mancala board game *bao* at Mwembebao. Apart from names associated with trees, there are also places such as Kuta la Tembo, which refers to the walled garden owned by an Indian family and according to stories home to one or more elephants (the name was already noted on the 1892 Baumann map, suggesting the place's significance). Nearby Kuta la Tembo, one can find the famous Raha Leo, 'happiness today', the only name in Ng'ambo given by the colonial authorities that still survives today. In addition, there is Baraste Kipande, whose name (meaning 'a piece of road') is an ironic comment on the ambitious but uncompleted colonial plans to build a road, which never went beyond the cutting of the ribbon in 1913.[30] The story behind the *mtaa* Kisiwandui, 'smallpox island,' refers to an islet in the creek that was reportedly used by the British administration as a quarantine for dhow crews that were suspected of carrying smallpox, a mortal disease that affected Zanzibar around the turn of the century.

Everyday economic activities

The toponymy of Ng'ambo also provides insights into the economic activities that took place in certain areas. From the place names we can learn that under the mango trees in Miembeni, in Mwembesanda, a type of cloth – *sanda* – was made, traditionally used to bury the dead. On the west side of Ng'ambo, towards Vikokotoni, fishermen would sit under the trees in Mwembetanga and mend their sails on the banks of the old creek (*tanga* means sail). Along the seashore south of Kikwajuni and Miembeni, fish traps were made in Mwembe Madema (*madema* means fish traps). In northern part, above Mchangani, there was an area where roof tiles were produced out of corrugated galvanized iron, called Mabatini. On the map of 1927 a wide open space can be identified called Zizi la Ng'ombe stretching from Mzeitini in the northwest to Baraste Kipande in the northeast, where there was once a cattle corral.

People-related

Old maps feature a number of names derived from the names of the pre-colonial landowners in Ng'ambo. Only one of them is still in use in the area: Biziredi, the name of an Arab woman, a plantation owner who financed the building of a mosque in the neighbourhood. The mosque continues to be referred to as the Biziredi Mosque, while the road in front of it is commonly known as the Biziredi Road. Kwa Haji Tumbo towards the northwest, is a name given to the location of the oldest market in Ng'ambo and means 'at Haji with the big belly'.

30 Garth Andrew Myers, "Naming and Placing the Other: Power and Urban Landscape in Zanzibar", in *Critical Toponymies: The Contested Politics of Place Naming*, eds. Lawrence D. Berg and Jani Vuolteenaho (London, Routledge, 2009), p. 92.

Legend

Trees

Natural features (other than trees)

Cultural-historical

Everyday economic activities

People-related

XXVI. Toponymy

XXVI. Toponymy

Fig 2.26: View of the creek from Mnazi Mmoja (date unknown)

Fig 2.27: View of Darajani Bridge (date unknown)

Fig 2.28: View of Creek Road in 2016

Fig 2.29: View of Darajani Street in 2016

Baraste Kipande 'a piece of road'
(*baraste* = road, *kipande* = piece)

Darajani 'at the bridge'
(*dara* = bridge, *ni* = at)

Gulioni 'at the market'
Gulio is an original Swahili word for market, used before the advent of the Arabic word *soko* (souk) and English-derived *marikiti* (market).

Kikwajuni 'at the small tamarind tree'
(*mkwaju* = tamarind tree)

Kisiwandui 'the smallpox island'
(*kisiwa* = island, *ndui* = smallpox)

Kisimamajongoo 'the well overrun with millipedes'
(*kisima* = well, *jongoo* = millipede)

Kuta la Tembo 'walls of the elephant'
(*kuta* = walls, *tembo* = elephant)

Kwa Haji Tumbo 'by Haji with the big belly'
(*kwa* = at/by, *tumbo* = belly)

Mapembeani 'at the big swings'
(*ma* = the big, *pembea* = swings)

Mayungwani 'at the coco-yam leaves place'
Yungwa is a coco-yam plant but the name relates more to the leaves, (hence the prefix 'ma') than the yams, called *majimbi* in Swahili. The tree is known by both names.

Mabatini 'at the tinsmiths' area'
(*mabati* = corrugated galvanized iron sheet)

Mbuyuni 'at the baobab tree'
(*mbuyu* = baobab tree)

Mbuyu Kidambwita 'the baobab tree of *Kidambwita* (a spirit)

Mbuyu Taifa 'the baobab-tree of the nation'
(*taifa* = nation)

Mchangani 'at the sandy area'
(*mchanga* = sand)

Mfenesi Mazizi 'the jackfruit tree with the big roots'
The roots of the tree grew above the ground, making the tree appear as if it was standing on them.

Michenzani 'at the tangerine trees'
(*chenza* = tangerine)

Miembeni 'at the mango trees'
(*mwembe* = mango)

Miembeni Jitini 'at the big tree in Miembeni'
(*jiti* = part of, or the entire big tree, whether dead or alive)

Miembeni Sakafuni the name refers to the tennis courts that used to be in the area
(*sakafu* = ground)

Mitiulaya 'the European trees'
The name indicates the manner in which the trees were arranged rather than the species.

Misufini 'at the silk-cotton/kapok trees'
(*misufi* = kapok tree)

Mkamasini 'at the large *mkamasi* tree'
(*mkamasi* = type of tree with a certain 'snotty' fruit)

Mlandege 'at the bird-feeding tree'
(*mla* = eat, *ndege* = bird)

Mnazi Mmoja 'one coconut tree' / 'the single coconut tree' (*mnazi* = coconut, *mmoja* = one)

According to the story the only one left at the former plantation after the 1875 hurricane.

Mtendeni 'at the date tree'
(*tende* = date)

Mwembebao 'the board-game tree'
(*bao* = is a particular type of board game)

Mwembe Kisonge 'the mango tree where they danced *kisonge*' (a type of *ngoma*)

Mwembe Madema 'the fish-trap mango tree'
(*dema* = fish trap)

Mwembeladu 'the *ladu* mango tree'
Ladu is a sort of a dry, round cake made of any cereal flower and sugar. It was sold beneath the mango tree referred to.

Mwemberikunda 'the *rikunda* mango tree'
The mango tree where people dance *rikunda*. *Rikunda* is a form of a dancing ritual to exorcise a spirit of that name.

Mwembesanda 'the *sanda* (-making place under the) mango tree' (*sanda* = type of cloth used to shroud the dead when buried)

The name indicates the place where the shrouds were made, since in Islam they have to be sewn directly on the body to be buried. It was an area in the neighbourhood where neighbours would convene to make the shroud for the deceased.

Mwembeshauri 'the advice mango tree'
(*shauri* = advice)

People practicing *shauri* under this tree were believed to be witches, since the meetings took place during late nights.

Mwembetanga 'the sail mango tree'
(*tanga* = sail)

Mzeitini 'at the *zaituni* trees'
Trees found in Zanzibar with mango-like fruits called *zaituni*.

Raha Leo 'happiness today'
(*raha* = happiness, *leo* = today)

Vikokotoni 'at the area of small pebbles'
(*kokoti* = small pebble, aggregate)

Pebbles from this area are said to have been used in the construction of Stone Town.

Zizi la Ng'ombe 'cattle coral'
(*zizi* = coral, *la* = of, *Ng'ombe*)

Places for Cultural Activities

Through the stories of older inhabitants, Ng'ambo emerges as a vibrant and energetic heart of Zanzibar Town and a place for all kinds of cultural entertainment. It is a part of area's heritage that is no longer visible in its urban landscape. Music and dance activities, which traditionally took place in open spaces in the neighborhoods, have either moved into hotels (where they more often than not cater for tourists visiting the island, rather than the local inhabitants), halls and other venues available in the city, or take place in private houses. This is not to say that music and dance have disappeared entirely from Ng'ambo, as there are still a small number of local bars in the area that hold *taarab* nights and other forms of performance. However, young people in search for a night out will, in general, go to Stone Town or to locations outside of the historic area.

The gradual disappearance of places for cultural activities from Ng'ambo can be seen as a consequence of ongoing urbanization, and a sign of the changing times – manifested in such everyday phenomena as (as was pointed out by the director of the DoURP) the fact that "women wear high heels nowadays, and you cannot dance on heals in the sandy streets". But it can also be seen as a long-term outcome of historical events such as the revolution, which had a lasting impact on the spatial, social and cultural layout of the area. The fact that the local population has become more conservative over the past three decades is also likely to play its role in the ways popular entertainment is being enacted in the urban realm.

The information presented on the map is not a complete representation of the cultural activities taking place in the area, nor does it reflect the heritage of the multiple communities that either used to live or whose descendants continue to live in Ng'ambo (for more information on the communities living in Ng'ambo see Chapter 1, p. 28). Most of the places mentioned in the map trace memories of informants who usually grew up in Ng'ambo around the time of the revolution. The picture that emerges from their stories is filled with a variety of *ngoma* (traditional dances), music playing in the streets, visits to the cinema, and pervading good spirits.

Fig 2.30: A street in Miembeni

One of the inhabitants referred to Miembeni as 'the happy streets of Ng'ambo', which seems perfectly to capture the spirit of the place. Through the stories, the mtaa *emerges as a lively but impoverished area, with bars that sold* pombe, *and where dance and music would draw people out into the streets.*

"African women were not allowed to dress as the royal families did, so they made their own dance and dress style with umbrellas. Their attitude was 'if they don't allow us, we'll do it our own way'. The umbrella was a sign of status [which] they used in their dance."

Farouque Abdela, fashion designer.

Fig 2.31: 'Music builds the nation', 1960s
The image represents a parade most likely taking place during the Revolution Day celebrations, commemorating the 1964 revolution.

Fig 2.32: Young girls performing an umbrella dance at school, 1980s

Fig 2.33: Umbrella dance performed during the Ng'ambo Tuitakayo visioning event in 2016

"In general people do not know much about the history of this island. So much of the history is lost. Most people do not know where Siti binti Saad is buried or where Bi Kidude used to live. Siti binti Saad is the first African woman to sign with Colombia Records in 1928, she should have her own monument here. People do not remember that Zanzibar used to be named 'Paris of the Indian Ocean'. The dresses that women used to wear when they were going to the Salum Beni Club were beautiful and fashionable. They really made an effort."

Farouque Abdela, fashion designer.

Fig 2.34: Siti binti Saad

Fig 2.35: Bi Kidude

Fig 2.36: Maryam Hamdani

Maryam Hamdani, a famous *taarab* player from Zanzibar and the founder of *Tausii Taarab*, who lives in Ng'ambo, considers the loss of spaces for cultural and creative activities as striking. In her opinion, this process is not only visible in the decreasing number of venues providing space for musical entertainment, stage performance or other forms for cultural activity. It is also a tendency that can be seen in schools, which once provided children with opportunities to perform, dance, play sports and learn music, and today no longer do.

For women, *taarab* played a similar role as football clubs did for men. Rivalry between female *taarab* groups was a central component of the *taarab* scene in Zanzibar. The performance of one such group – named Royal Air Force – simulated a plane journey. The leader of the group played the role of the pilot, the 'piloti', while the remaining women were dressed as flight attendants. The 'piloti' would start each performance with an introduction imitating a take-off.

"I was not a good singer, but I told the stories; I introduced the band. The story was as if we arrived by plane, and we were all dressed as flight attendants. In my time, taarab *was more active, the public would participate in the event. Now the audience is more passive, there is not a lot of dancing anymore."*

Saada Jaffer, former leader of Royal Air Force, Kisiwandui.

"When I got married I became a member of the taarab *group Royal Air Force, then Akwan Saffa, later Kikundi cha Taifa. There was great rivalry between the different groups, but the rivalry was only in the songs. Friends among different groups existed, but the identification with the individual groups was strong."*

Fatma Mohammed Bambam, Mlandege.

Annotations to the map

CCM Social Hall

Local restaurant with dance and music performances. CCM is an abbreviation for Chama Cha Mapinduzi, the name of one of the two major political parties in Zanzibar.

Gymkhana Club

Local restaurant with dance and music performances, *taarab* nights and television screenings in the evenings.

Mtendeni Maulid

The Mtendeni Maulid Ensemble performs a Sufi religious devotion called Maulidi ya Homu. They practice in the madrassa marked on the map. According to the members of the group, every evening during the rehearsals people from the neighbourhood gather around the building to watch the performance. The group performs at different venues around the world and more locally in Zanzibar at weddings and in hotels or at festivals such as the Zanzibar International Film Festival and the music festival Sauti Za Busara.

Tausi Taarab

World-renowned *taarab* group constituting entirely of women and performing under the leadership of Maryam Hamdani. The house indicated on the map is Maryam Hamdani's house, which serves as a kind of women's centre. Women come here to learn *taarab*, to socialize and at times to seek financial support. When Hamdani started Tausi Taarab, women were lining up in front of the house at 8am in hope of joining the group. This reassured her that providing women with the opportunity to play music was the right thing to do to.

Fig 2.37: CCM Social Hall

Fig 2.38: Gymkhana Club

Fig 2.39: Mtendeni Maulid
House where the group rehearses and performs.

Legend

Still present

No longer present

XXVII. Places for Cultural Activities

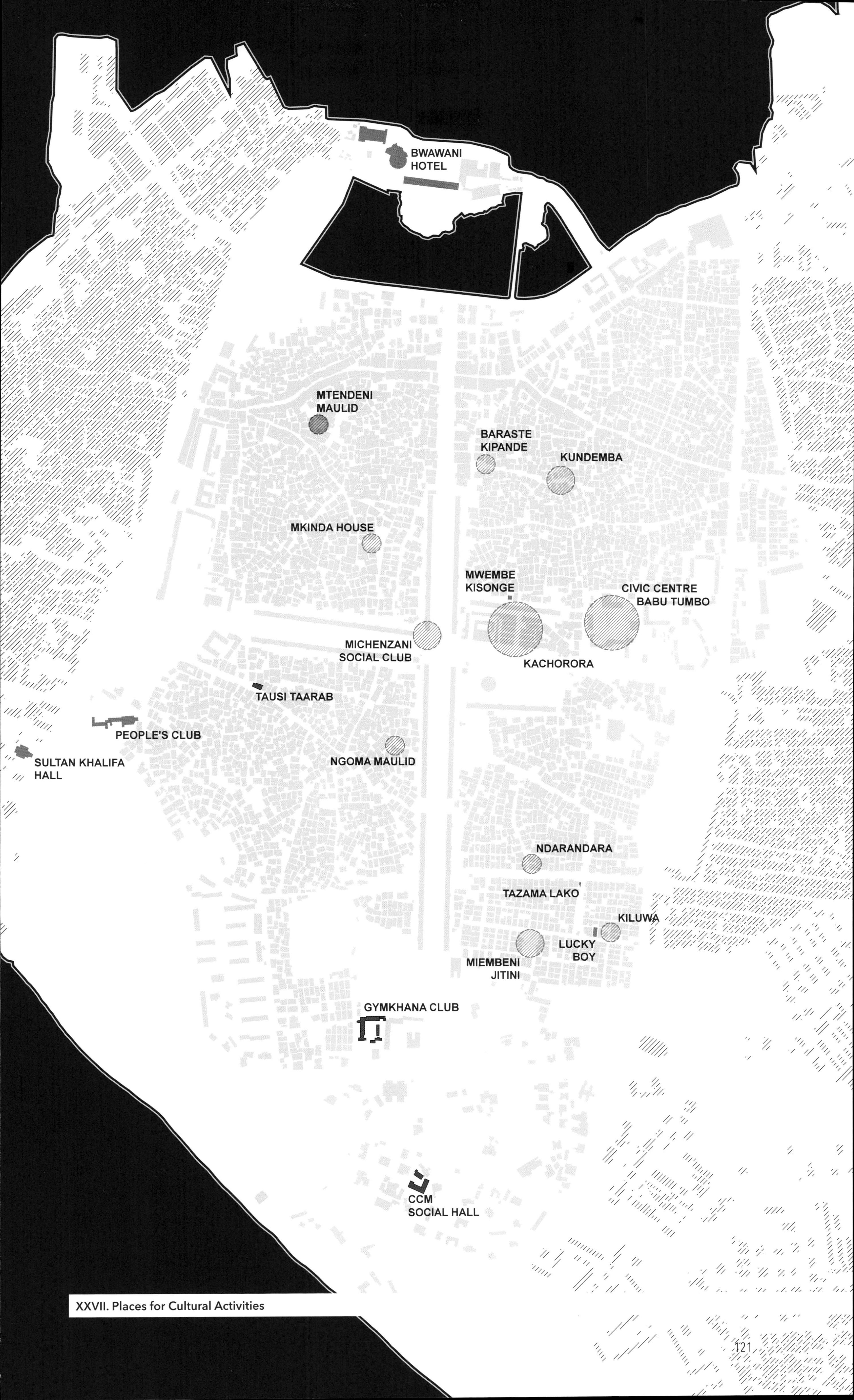

XXVII. Places for Cultural Activities

Babu Tumbo

Not a drive-in cinema, but a driving cinema. Babu Tumbo was a man who owned a lorry that functioned as a cinema. Silent movies were played on a white screen or sheet that was mounted on the back of the lorry. The vehicle was stationed in Raha Leo, but Babu Tumbo would drive his cinema on wheels to the *shamba* (rural areas) where he screened educational movies for the people.

Baraste Kipande

Part of a street that was planned in 1913, also used as space for dancing traditional *ngoma*.

Bwawani Hotel

Government-run hotel which opened in 1976 and was a regular venue for music and dance performances by local groups.

Civic Centre

A popular place, not only for people from this part of town. In the evenings people would sit outside in the open space in front of the Civic Centre and listen to the Voice of Zanzibar broadcast through speakers. In addition to regular broadcasts, the results of university examinations were also announced on the radio, a tradition maintained to this day. The Civic Centre also hosted a cinema, the only one that ever existed in Ng'ambo. The other three cinemas were located in Stone Town – the Majestic, Cine-Afrique (previously the Sultana) and Empire. Today the former Civic Centre has lost its communal importance. The open space in front of the building has been fenced off, and the barely accessible premises are home to a newly opened recording studio.

Kachorora

The 'narrow streets', where people used to dance *kiluwa*, a dance of the Manyema tribe from the mainland.

Kiluwa

Area referred to by people as *kiluwa* after a type of ngoma that was danced there. An indoor dancing club called Lucky Boy used to be nearby.

Kundemba

According to people from the area, this was formerly a large open space where *pombe* (local beer) was sold and people played *bomu* the popular *ngoma* from Zanzibar. The locally known musician Rashidi Kigogo performed here as well.

Miembeni Jitini

This large open space, named Jitiulaya after the large tree that shades it, was created as a part of the redevelopment scheme for Miembeni. The remains of a watering place for animals are still visible at the centre of the space. Today the area is used for various activities: there is a car workshop and some smaller *dukas*, a *maskan* and space for children to play. According to local women, the area was once used for dancing, playing the popular brass band *beni* music and *taarab*.

Early influences from military brass bands (introduced with the German and British military operations taking place on the East African coast in late 19th century) were transformed into a new dance style known as the beni ngoma. *The dance and steps imitate military drills and the accompanying brass bands. It became a more innovative form of the traditional* ngoma.[31]

Michenzani Social Club

The club was founded by people of African descent and opened its doors in 1954 as the first club to be started in the area. It hosted jazz bands, among which the famous jazz band Salum Beni was a regular performer. The highly popular *taarab* musician Bakari Abeid was also a regular performer at the club. According to some people the club was a place for the more well-to-do inhabitants of the area and was influenced by British music and dances.

Fig 2.40: Bwawani Hotel

Fig 2.41: Miembeni Jitini

[31] Stephen H. Martin, "Brass Bands and the Beni Phenomenon in Urban East Africa", *African Music*, 7, no. 2 (1991), pp. 72-81.

Mkinda House

Special venue or place for performing *mkinda*, a form of female puberty initiation ritual. This form of initiation was created by urban Zanzibari women directly after the abolition of slavery. The traditional initiation ritual, performed by older women in East Africa in the 19th century, was *unyago*. During the ritual young girls were taught about female sexuality and morality. *Unyago* rituals were never performed publicly. In Zanzibar, *unyago* was predominantly practiced by slave women of African descent. *Mkinda* became an initiation ritual for children of mixed Arab and African parentage.

"The dances associated with mkinda were public celebrations that marked the transformation of young girls into women, and simultaneously celebrations of the historical power of women's sexuality to create bridges between the island's diverse ethnic and cultural communities, particularly between Africans and Arabs".[32]

Mwembe Kisonge

'The tree where they danced *kisonge*', *ngoma* from the Manyema tribe in which men and women dance together.

Ndarandara

An open space used for dancing *ndarandara* a traditional dance of the Wazaramu tribe from the mainland. The locally famous Zanzibar Jazz Band performed here regularly.

Ngoma Maulid

Open space where people danced *maulid*.
During a *maulidi* performance, readings of the life story of the Prophet Mohammed take place. In Zanzibar the *maulidi* performance can take two forms. During the month of the birth of the Prophet and on other religious occasions, *maulidi* performances are public events taking place in large open spaces allowing for large gatherings. There is no music, but the readings of the chapter are accompanied by sung poems. During weddings, the readings are more improvised and are accompanied by eight frame drums of different sizes.[33]

The word ngoma*, in its narrowest sense, refers to a drum, but it also serves to describe any event with music and dance. Countless varieties of* ngoma *can be distinguished, based on the ethnicity and gender of the participants, the region of its origin and its function. Certain features of local* ngoma *have been incorporated into* taarab *music in Zanzibar and the overlap between the two is quite complex. In general,* ngoma *events are characterized by spectator participation.* Taarab*, in its most traditional form, is a more passive type of entertainment, although modern* taarab *has become more interactive and often involves participation of the public through dance.*[34]

People's Club

Music and dance venue mostly for the more affluent inhabitants of the area, began after the revolution and remained open until the 1970s.

Sultan Khalifa Hall / Karume House

The venue served as an assembly and performance hall open to the public until the revolution. In the words of Maryam Hamdani, the interior of the hall "was just like European theatres". After the revolution the building was taken over by TVZ and renamed Karume House. It is no longer open to the public, a fact regarded as a great loss by people remembering the times before the revolution.

Tazama Lako

At this *maskan* men would drink a local liquor called *mtindi wa mitindi*. The story goes that whenever people passed by and frowned on their activities, the drinkers would suggest that the passer-by 'mind his/her own [business]'. The place is still referred to as *Tazama Lako* ('mind your own...').

The name of the liquor mtindi wa mitindi *literally translates as 'the yoghurt of yoghurts', whereas in its common use it is understood as 'the mother of all local brews'. The local brew had many street names including:* gongo *'the big stick',* tende *'the dates' and* mtindi *'yoghurt'.*

Fig 2.42: Ndarandara

Now a wakf *association building; once headquarters of YASU (Young African Social Union).*

Fig 2.43: Ngoma Maulid

An open space formerly used to dance maulid. *Open spaces as well as green spaces and trees in Ng'ambo are rapidly disappearing due to uncontrolled urban development.*

32 Laura Fair, "Remaking Fashion in the Paris of the Indian Ocean: Dress, Performance and Cultural Construction of a Cosmopolitan Zanzibari Identity", in *Fashioning Africa: Power and the Politics of Dress*, ed. Jean Allman (Bloomington, Indiana University Press, 2004), p. 22.

33 Janet Topp Fargion, "The Music of Zenj: Arab-African Crossovers in the Music of Zanzibar", *Journal des Africanistes*, 72 (2002), pp. 203-212.

34 For more on *taarab* and *ngoma* reference Janet Topp Fargion's work in the bibliography, including Janet Topp Fargion "The Role of Women in Taarab in Zanzibar: an Historical Examination of a Process of 'Africanisation'", *The World of Music*, 35, no. 2 (1993), p. 111.

Cinema in Zanzibar Town

Cinema was often brought up as a favourite pastime. People say that, where there is now a carpark for *dala dala*, near the Darajani Market, there was once a noticeboard displaying an overview of times, names and locations of all the movies running in town. Back in the day, everybody went to the cinema - as one of the elders living in Kisiwandui said. There were three cinemas in Stone Town: the Majestic, Empire and Cine Afrique, and one in the Civic Centre in Raha Leo. On Sunday it was 'one shilling go round', meaning that all tickets cost a shilling. During the week the price would depend on the seat. Visits to the cinema went into a decline after the introduction of TV into the area in the late 1970s. Today there are several cinemas in Zanzibar Town, but screenings are not regular. The Empire Cinema doesn't exist anymore, the Cine Afrique has been renovated and turned into offices, while the Majestic in Vuga is in a dire condition, although, thanks to its caretaker, movies are still being screened there for a small group of devoted fans.

Fig 2.44: The Majestic Cinema in Vuga

Fig 2.45: The Sultana Cinema in Malindi
The cinema was renamed Cine Afrique in 1964.

A note on trees

by Salim Said Salim

I can recall how I enjoyed walking for almost half a kilometre in one of the streets of Miembeni at midday without the sun's rays burning any part of my body. This area had about fifty trees on each side, like Maruhubi, outside Zanzibar Town, Bungi to the south of Zanzibar and Boma Road in Tabora on the mainland.

For many years the mango tree has had a special significance to the people of Zanzibar. It is very unfortunate that nowadays we don't think twice before cutting them down. In Zanzibar, as in other parts of the United Republic, people do not take time to contemplate the fact that our country once had a close connection with trees, and that this is why many areas have derived their identity and their names from trees.

It used to be a tradition for the people of Zanzibar – as was the case in many parts of the East African coast – to name localities after the flora of the place, especially the mango tree. According to statistics, Tanzania ranks seventh in the world with the highest number of mango trees and with more than thirty varieties of the fruit in different shapes, sizes and flavours. Some of these varieties have disappeared and the present generation does not know about them, which I find very sad.

Zanzibar and Pemba have more than 100 places named after the mango tree. The Zanzibar Municipality alone has more than 30 places whose names start with Mwembe. Just to mention a few: Mwembe Mimba (a place under which an old woman by the name of Mwanajuma used to sit). She gave herbs to women who failed to conceive after years of being married. The story goes that most of the women who used her herbs succeeded in falling pregnant. Then there is Mwembeshauri (a mango tree of consultancy): under this tree, elders of 70 years and more arbitrated in disputes between married couples, family members and neighbours. Other places carrying the name of the mango tree are Mwembetanga (under which people did the canvas art work, especially for dhows); Mwembe Njuugu (groundnut mango), under which there was a popular groundnut market; Mwembebeni, a popular entertainment spot, with bands playing under its shade; Mwembe Matarumbeta (a trumpet mango) under which the Police Band used to rehearse. Other examples include Mwembe Mchomeke, Memberikunda, Mwembeladu, Mwembemadema, Mwembedodo, Mwembekidundo, and Mwembesanda.

But gone are the days when mango trees were scattered all over the islands, including in Zanzibar Town. Many of them, as with other trees such as the coconut and baobab, have been cut down to make way for housing and other building projects. I think it is high time that the people of Zanzibar considered the harm they are doing to the flora they inherited from their ancestors, or history will not forgive them.

Fig 2.46: A tree-lined avenue in Kikwajuni

Public Recreation

Public recreation has played an immense role in the lives of the various communities intersecting in Ng'ambo. While open spaces are generally disappearing from Ng'ambo's urban fabric under the pressure of rapid development and land grabbing, the two major sports grounds - Mnazi Mmoja and Mbuyuni/Mchangani - have so far remained untouched. The roots of public recreation in Ng'ambo go back to the 19th century, which is when the first mentions of sports grounds can be found on the maps (*see* Chapter 1, maps IV, V, VII, X and XIV). While the Mnazi Mmoja ground has been continuously in use since the late 19th century, other sports venues identified by people from the area such as Miembeni Mpirani (once a football field) or the tennis grounds Miembeni Sakafuni, are today only a memory. The Mao Tse-Tung Stadium (dismantled in the late 1980s) previously known as the Seyyid Khalifa Sports Grounds, a sandy field used by boys and men from local neighbourhoods to play football, is currently awaiting restoration.

Since its introduction into Zanzibar in the late 1870s, football has been a central social experience for men. In colonial times, football played an important role in the process of building community identity and in challenging existing authority and political order. For many young men, it was the only possibility available to them to improve their status and position. The communal importance of football and its accompanying feelings of hope, and of admiration for the players, remains uncontested. Neighbourhood football clubs continue to be focal points of many social activities; young men who can boast about their football skills enjoy a widespread recognition in the area, and there is a strong sense of belonging among the supporters of the respective football teams from Ng'ambo.

From the late 1940s Ng'ambo was also provided with a number of playgrounds for children living in the area, which in contrast to the major sports grounds have not stood the test of time. Playgrounds once located in Mwembetanga, Raha Leo and near the Jamhuri Gardens were easily accessible communal spaces. The only remaining playground in the area is located in the Jamhuri Gardens and as with the funfair in Kariakoo and the playground in Forodhani Gardens, is a fenced-off space entered for a fee.

Fig 2.47: Football game at Mao Tse-Tung Stadium

Fig 2.48: Cycling race (surroundings of Mnazi Mmoja) in the 1970s

Fig 2.49: Bullfights at Mao Tse-Tung Stadium in the 1980s

Legend

STILL PRESENT

Sports and recreation grounds

Playgrounds

NO LONGER PRESENT

Sports and recreation grounds

Playgrounds

XXVIII. Public Recreation

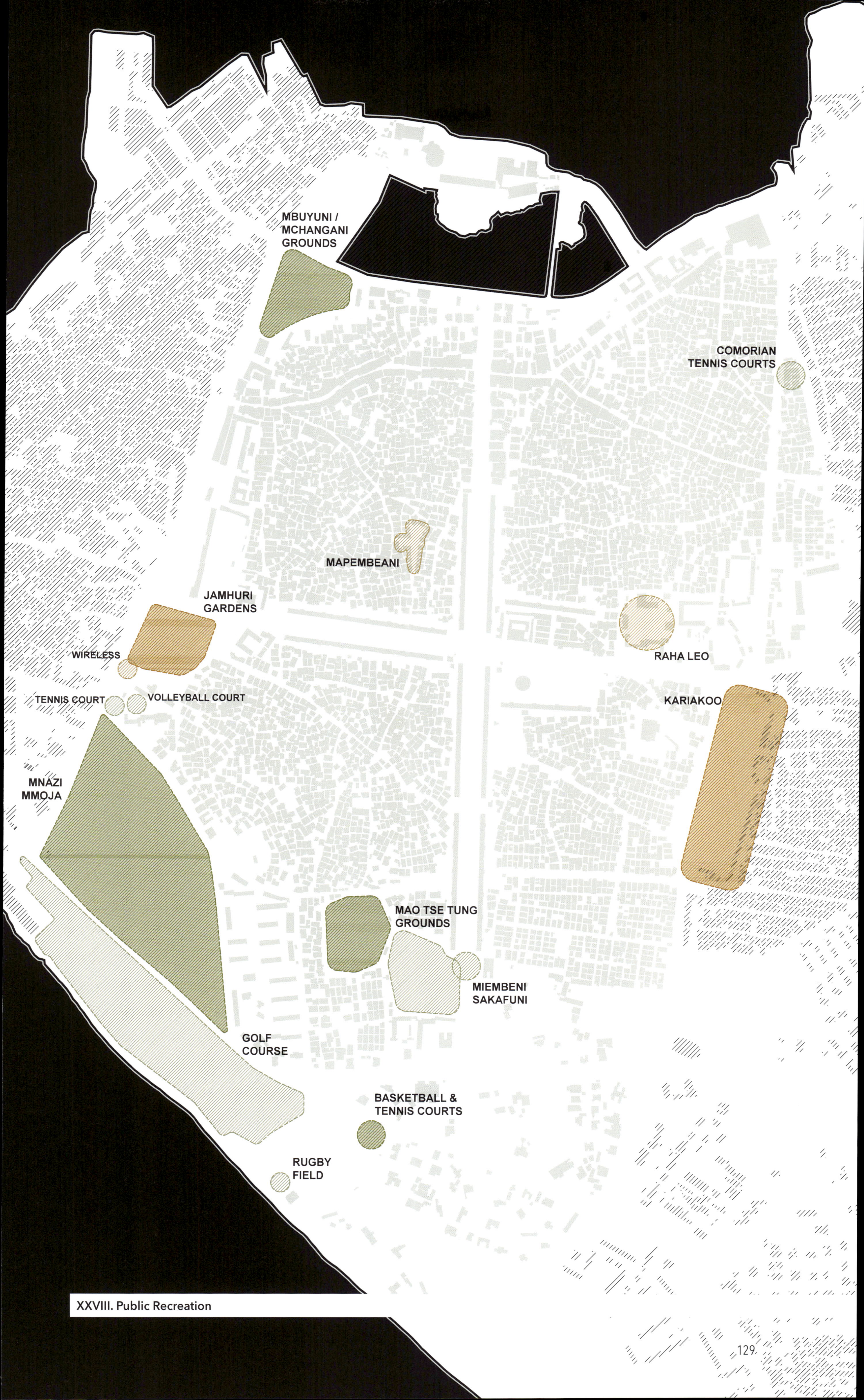

XXVIII. Public Recreation

Fig 2.50: Location of football team pitches on Mnazi Mmoja grounds

The continuing importance of football is manifested in a shared feeling of responsibility for the informal football pitches associated with various teams to be found at the Mnazi Mmoja grounds. Several teams use the Mnazi Mmoja grounds for practice. The map shows the approximate location of their pitches. Each pitch is known by a different name, and while some of them are either out of use or are no longer used by the same teams, they continue to be referred to by their original names.

According to the famous coach Abdulghani Msoma, who established the football club Small Simba in 1972, the quality of football in Zanzibar is diminishing, because of the overwhelming number of teams and clubs and the scarcity of available financial support.

Fig 2.51: Football players at Mnazi Mmoja

Fig 2.52: The Weight Lifting Association at Mnazi Mmoja

Mapembeani

Mapembeani ('at the big swings') was a part of the British housing scheme - the planned urban transformation of Mwembetanga by the British land officer Eric Dutton started in July 1947 (*see* Chapter 1, pp. 48-51). The playground included a slide, a large and small merry-go-round, swings located in the north-western corner and a seesaw to the north. Both merry-go-rounds were powered by hand. Mapembeani was the first playground that was ever built in Ng'ambo and attracted visitors even from outside of the area. According to older inhabitants there were groups of children wandering around Ng'ambo in search of new places to play every day, and for a long time Mapembeani was one of their favourite destinations. Since the playground was located in the middle of an area that was at the time regarded as a native quarter, children playing in Mwembetanga were predominantly of African, Arab, Comorian or Indian descent. It is not known whether children of British descent and of the Indian upper-classes played there as well. Some say that the playground was originally built for the children of British civil servants. However, the older inhabitants of Mwembetanga differ quite markedly on this matter in their stories. Similar merry-go-rounds were built at Raha Leo and in Kisiwandui close to one of the offices of the Cable and Wireless telegraph company, which lent its name to the playground commonly referred to as the Wireless. The playground in Mwembetanga was dismantled in 1968, due to lack of maintenance. Some claim that the unsupervised equipment resulted in a large number of injuries. This might also be the reason why the playgrounds at Raha Leo and Wireless - which were located nearby dispensaries - were maintained a little longer (until 1970). The empty plots left by the playgrounds in Raha Leo and Kisiwandui are no longer discernible, but that of Mapembeani in Mwembetanga remains undeveloped and is currently used by children for playing football.[35]

"When I was younger I used to play netball a lot. This was a very popular sport for girls; it still is today. At Gymkhana, they play netball nowadays."

Frida Salma, Kikwajuni.

"Now there are fewer open spaces for children to play than before. Ideally, there should be a playground in every neighbourhood. Now parents have to travel very far."

Older woman, Kikwajuni.

LAYERS OF HISTORY IN MAPEMBEANI

Fig 2.53: Layers of history at Mapembeani
Map showing visible, semi-visible and hidden history at Mapembeani.

Fig 2.54: Kariakoo Funfair
Located outside the project area, but still in use today (owned by Zanzibar Social Security Fund).

Fig 2.55: Boys playing football at Mapembeani

Fig 2.56: Jamhuri Gardens
The gardens in Kisimamajongoo play an important role as space for social interaction and recreation, often frequented by university students, who use the space for after-school gatherings.

[35] Mia Callenberg, *Hidden Stories and Urban Values in Zanzibar. History and Heritage-Based Regeneration of Ng'ambo: a pilot study of Mapembeani*. Master's thesis (Gothenburg, Chalmers University of Technology, 2015).

Places for Social Interaction

A large part of the day-to-day life in Zanzibar takes place in the streets. Men and women occupy the outdoor spaces in different ways. However, there are places within the city where people cross paths regardless of their gender, both on a daily basis or for special occasions. Social surroundings other than home and work-place are considered as 'third places', providing the community with the opportunity for various forms of social interaction.[36] Through the narratives of storytellers from the area, a number of historical and existing 'third places' were identified in Ng'ambo: mosques, markets, clubhouses, community halls, traffic nodes and water taps. The places for social interaction identified differ substantially in their nature and function. What they do have in common is the important role they either played or continue to play in the social life of the local community.

Legend

STILL PRESENT
- Community halls
- Football clubhouses
- Markets
- Mosques
- Traffic nodes
- Water taps

NO LONGER PRESENT
- Community halls
- Football clubhouses
- Markets
- Traffic nodes
- Water taps

XXIX. Places for Social Interaction

[36] The term 'third places' is used by, among others, Ray Oldenburg. See for example: Ray Oldenburg, "Our vanishing third places", *Planning Commissioners Journal*, 25, no. 4 (1997), pp. 6-10.

XXIX. Places for Social Interaction

Community halls and clubs

Community halls and clubs once played an important role in the social life of the different ethnic communities in Ng'ambo. Buildings that once hosted the community halls and clubs can still be found in the area, but are now adapted for new use.

Bohora Community Club (Gymkhana)

The complex and the adjoining grounds were used by the Bohora community as an assembly hall and for sports. The building later housed the EACROTANAL (East African Centre for Research on Oral Traditions and African National Languages) and today houses the East African Kiswahili Commission.

Bwawani Hotel

A government-owned hotel under the revolutionary regime, located on the port-side of the Malindi neighbourhood. For many years it remained one of the few hotels on the island, with a bar and restaurant serving as a meeting place for the local upper classes and foreigners.[37] When it ceased to function as a hotel, the grounds around the swimming pool were turned into a music club for young people and a gym, whereas the main building was used by the government for offices. The entire complex is currently being redeveloped.

Golf Club

A privately owned club run by Europeans during colonial times and accessible only to a privileged segment of the public. Today the same building hosts a local bar.

Kwa Pa Puri

A community hall for Indian people in Kikwajuni. Today used as a fire station.

Sir Tayabali Hall

Built in the early 20th century as a club for the Indian population by the Zanzibari philanthropist Tayabali Karimjee, and serving until the revolution as a place for performances and dance. After the revolution the building housed the People's Club, a famous music club for (mainly) the upper classes. After 1977 it was turned into the House of Representatives. Today the building houses the Ministry of Culture, Sports and Tourism.

Fig 2.57: Former location of the Golf Club

Fig 2.58: Former location of the Sir Tayabali Hall

Fig 2.59: Former location of the Bohora Community Club

Fig 2.60: Bwawani Complex in 2009

[37] Garth Andrew Myers, "Representing Postcolonial Zanzibar in Contested Literary, Cultural and Political Geographies", in *The Postcolonial World*, eds. Jyotsna Singh and David D. Kim (London, Routledge, 2016), p. 233.

Football team clubhouses

With the growing importance of football in Ng'ambo, teams from the respective neighbourhoods were provided with clubhouses which became important gathering places for their members and supporters. Men would meet at the clubhouses to play *bao* and checkers or to gossip. According to Laura Fair, "clubs and clubhouses provided the space for young boys to grow into men, and above all else they created the opportunity for men to establish and develop the friendships that would last them throughout their lives".[38] A number of clubhouses such as Miembeni Football Club and Ujamaa Sports Club have maintained their original functions, whereas others, like the old clubhouse of the Kisimamajongoo Sports Club and Vikokotoni Football Club, are no longer in use.

Markets

Markets are important nodes of social interaction for sellers, buyers and visitors. The biggest market in this part of town is the Darajani Market, located at the border of Stone Town and Ng'ambo where there was once a bridge crossing the creek. The market thrives with all kinds of businesses and caters for most needs of the inhabitants of Zanzibar Town. It has also become a major attraction for tourists visiting Stone Town. The Kwa Haji Tumbo Market, located in the north-eastern part of Ng'ambo, was named as the oldest and, once, the biggest market. It is still in use, but is now much smaller in size and sells primarily dried fish. Markets that no longer exist are the Maziwa Market (where milk was sold), the Soko Ya Samaki (a fish market) (*see* Chapter 1, maps IV and V) and the Gulioni Market. In colonial times there was also a market providing imported goods for the Europeans living in Zanzibar called the Good Luck Market.

Fig 2.61: Miembeni Sports Club

Fig 2.62: Kisimamajongo Sports Club

Fig 2.63: Kwa Haji Tumbo Market

The oldest market in Ng'ambo that is still in use (date unknown).

Fig 2.64: Gulioni Market (date unknown)

Fig 2.65: Kwa Haji Tumbo Market in 2016

Fig 2.66: Darajani Market in 2016

[38] Laura Fair, "Kickin' It: Leisure, Politics and Football in Colonial Zanzibar, 1900s-1950s", *Africa: Journal of the International African Institute*, 67, no. 2 (1997), p. 243.

Mosques

Located at the centre of each *mtaa*, mosques serve as the town's public lounges. There are more mosques per capita than any other social facilities in town. They serve not only as places of worship but also as centres of religious education, areas of daily ritual, social interaction and as meeting places for their respective congregations.

Fig 2.67: Men gathering at the mosque

Traffic nodes

Due to their strategic importance for local transport and traffic, *dala dala* stations and roundabouts were indicated as important places for social interaction.

In Zanzibar public transport is typically provided by *dala dala*, which are, in contrast to the minibuses found on the mainland, converted pick-up trucks fitting up to 22 people and operating on routes across the whole island.

Fig 2.68: A *dala dala*

Of the roundabouts, the Michenzani Roundabout is particularly notable. A number of small shops and restaurants opened in its vicinity, attracting people to the area throughout the day. The roundabout also figures prominently in the political landscape of Ng'ambo, hosting the *maskani* of two major and opposing political parties, the ruling CCM (Chama Cha Mapinduzi) and the CUF (Civic United Front), across the road from each other. Both *maskani* are referred to as *kahawa maskani*, meaning the maskani where coffee is served. The Keep-Left Roundabout was also mentioned as an erstwhile gathering point, taking its name from a traffic sign that used to be there.

Water taps

Public water taps, *mfreji*, while no longer in use, were identified as historically important gathering places for women, providing them with the opportunity to meet in public spaces. Over the course of time the water taps were assigned names, which continue to be used by the older generation when referring to the individual taps. The identified water taps include: Mfereji Wa Kiambazani 'the water tap by the wall'; Mfereji Maringo 'the slow-dripping water tap'; Mfereji Wa Shimo 'the tap at the hole' and Mfereji Kwawambwa 'Kwawamba's water tap'.

Fig 2.69: Mfereji Wa Shimo, 'the tap at the hole'

Fig 2.70: Mfereji Wa Kiambazini, 'the water tap in the wall'

"The Michenzani Roundabout is actually the centre of the city. Commercial activity along the Michenzani Roundabout has increased substantially in past years, most notably the container shops in Raha Leo which come alive during the evenings. All kinds of different people come here, but mainly younger ones. This is actually one of the few fun places in Ng'ambo that we can go to in the evenings."

Farid Himid, expert on culture and history of Ng'ambo and tourist guide.

Fig 2.71: Michenzani Roundabout

Shops, restaurants and street-food stands are other important places for social interaction. Some of them have existed in the area for decades, and are known as family businesses or as places selling the best food or product of particular type in the city. One such place is Maharuki's halwa shop, near the Mtendeni Mosque, where the family has plied their trade for decades making sweet halwa renowned throughout the city.

Fig 2.72: Local restaurant

Fig 2.73: Local restaurant

Handcrafts

Production of handcrafts is not only an important economic activity, but also plays a significant role in maintaining local customs and traditions. The presence of artisans and craftsmen in the public realm in Ng'ambo has generally diminished over the years, as they have become confined to specific areas or have moved from the streets into the interiors of houses and shops. In some places handcrafts are still practiced today, whereas in others they endure in place names and in the living memory of Ng'ambo's older inhabitants.

One of the neighbourhoods with the highest concentration of crafts is Gulioni, where tinsmiths and ironworkers continue the production and sale of objects. In the past the neighbourhood consisted largely of craftsmen's tin sheds. The sheds were at a certain point also used as laundry facilities by the Baniyani Indian community. Boat builders have also remained in Gulioni and continue to do their business in the area, despite the re-location caused by the construction of the Bank of Tanzania. The main centre for the sale of timber and woodwork is located in Mitiulaya.

Names such as Misufini, Batini or Mwembe Madema are toponymical remainders of crafts that were practiced in these places. Misufini indicates the location where mattresses filled with cotton wool from kapok fruit, were made (used largely by the poor). Batini or Mabatni (plural) is where corrugated iron sheets were produced, and traditional fishing traps were once made in Mwembe Madema. The names Mapipa Ya Ngozi (area in which shoemakers worked and where animal skins were dried) and Kumbaro (referring to the Indian community traditionally engaged in pot making) have not endured in the toponymy of Ng'ambo, but remain in the living memory of older generations.

Two of Ng'ambo's neighbourhoods are closely associated with specific crafts. Mchangani, known for the embroidering of gowns, and Kikwajuni known for the cultivation of jasmine. For a long time, gown embroidery in Mchangani was a trade conducted by just one family. The well-known Mzee Marin took over the family business from his father. In the past, the embroidering was done in front of the Marin family home. The quality of the final product was so high that it gained widespread recognition, attracting buyers not only from the island, but also from outside of Zanzibar.

Jasmine is seen as a powerful aphrodisiac, used by Zanzibari women particularly on their wedding days. Jasmin flowers are spread on beds, dining tables or arranged in *kikuba*, a small bouquet used as an adornment in the hair or placed above the female pubic area. Binti Humudi, who lived in Kikwajuni, was famous for her production of *kikuba*, which she sold to women from the entire area.

Legend

Still present

No longer present

XXX. Handcrafts

XXX. Handcrafts

Fig 2.74: Sheds in Gulioni

A number of sheds for tinsmiths were once located along this road, of which only this one remains. Ironwork began in the area after revolution; before then the sheds were used by Indians as laundry facilities.

Fig 2.75: Tinsmiths in Gulioni

Fig 2.76: Timber sale and woodwork in Mitiulaya

Fig 2.77: Boatbuilding and repair in Kinazini, Gulioni

Fig 2.78: Basket manufacturers (date unknown)

Fig 2.79: Mattress-making in Misufini (date unknown)

Zanzibar Bus Routes and Urban Heritage

Excerpt from the unpublished book *What a Zanzibar!*, by Mwalim A. Mwalim, former director general of Stone Town Conservation Department Authorities

'Zanzibar has a unique system of public transport. There are no major routes connecting one rural district to another, but all key rural destinations are directly connected by separate routes to the town. Unlike usual international practice, route numbers are displayed only on wooden plaques in the front and rear of the buses (or sometimes pick-up vehicles) serving those roads and not on signs along the respective highways themselves. It may safely be said, then, that there are no route numbers in Zanzibar, only bus numbers. Or that those two could be used interchangeably for reference.

The white numbers on a black background (or the reverse) are therefore bi-functional. Firstly, they mark the route numbers and, secondly, they declare the main destination (which is usually but not necessarily the final one). Because all the routes commonly start at one point in one place - Zanzibar Town for the Unguja Island; or Wete, Chake or Mkoani Towns for the sister island of Pemba - sometimes the conductor has to shout the several villages such transport would pass through on the way to its final destination, which is normally helpful for passengers new to the relevant route. Surprisingly, even the most illiterate passengers are able easily to recognize the numbers and correlate them to destinations. I know no reported case of someone boarding a wrong bus through illiteracy.

This numbering system is a legacy in itself. People strongly associate themselves with the numbers of the routes leading to their respective villages. Those sharing a common (bus/route) number identify themselves as one sub-community, so much so that the entire population of Zanzibar could be generally referred to by the numbers 1 to 11 for Unguja Island, and 1 to 24 for Pemba. Later, a closer kinship develops within those sub-communities, thereby creating a sub-culture. It is an interesting phenomenon I have never seen elsewhere.

In town, these sub-cultures concentrate along their entry routes, gradually fusing together to finally merge at the bus terminus in the city centre. Zanzibar's urban neighbourhoods are therefore like clans of those sub-cultures, within which residents from the same villages subdivide into separate sub-neighbourhoods. This makes the city an harmonious representative concentration of villages centered on the route of entry into town. Imagine a large terrestrial octopus with the tentacles as the sub-cultures, urban neighbourhoods along the routes of entry, and the head as the city centre, and you have created a clear image of this ingenious spontaneous planning inspired by these primitive-looking buses through their routes.

Later I saw somewhat similar vehicles in Ghana, the Philippines and the Caribbean, but none of them had played that wonderful role in the fusion of urban societies and unification of rural ones as do these modified Zanzibar omnibuses. They are called mbavu za mbwa *('dogs' ribs' in Swahili) in ridicule, but these airy buses have forged a national bond so strong that no political establishment can ever, and in my opinion will ever, match!*

Fig 2.80: Riding in a *dala dala*

Legend

1. Nungwi/Donge/Mkokotoni
2. Mangapwani/Bumbwini
3. Dole/Mndo
4. Dunga/Uzini/Mchangani
5. Kiboje/Ndagaa
6. Chaka/Uroa
7. Rumba/Bweleo
8. Ungujaukuu
9. Bwejuu/Paje/Jambiani
10. Makunduchi/ Kizimkazi
11. Ndijani/Binguni

XXXI. Zanzibar Bus Routes

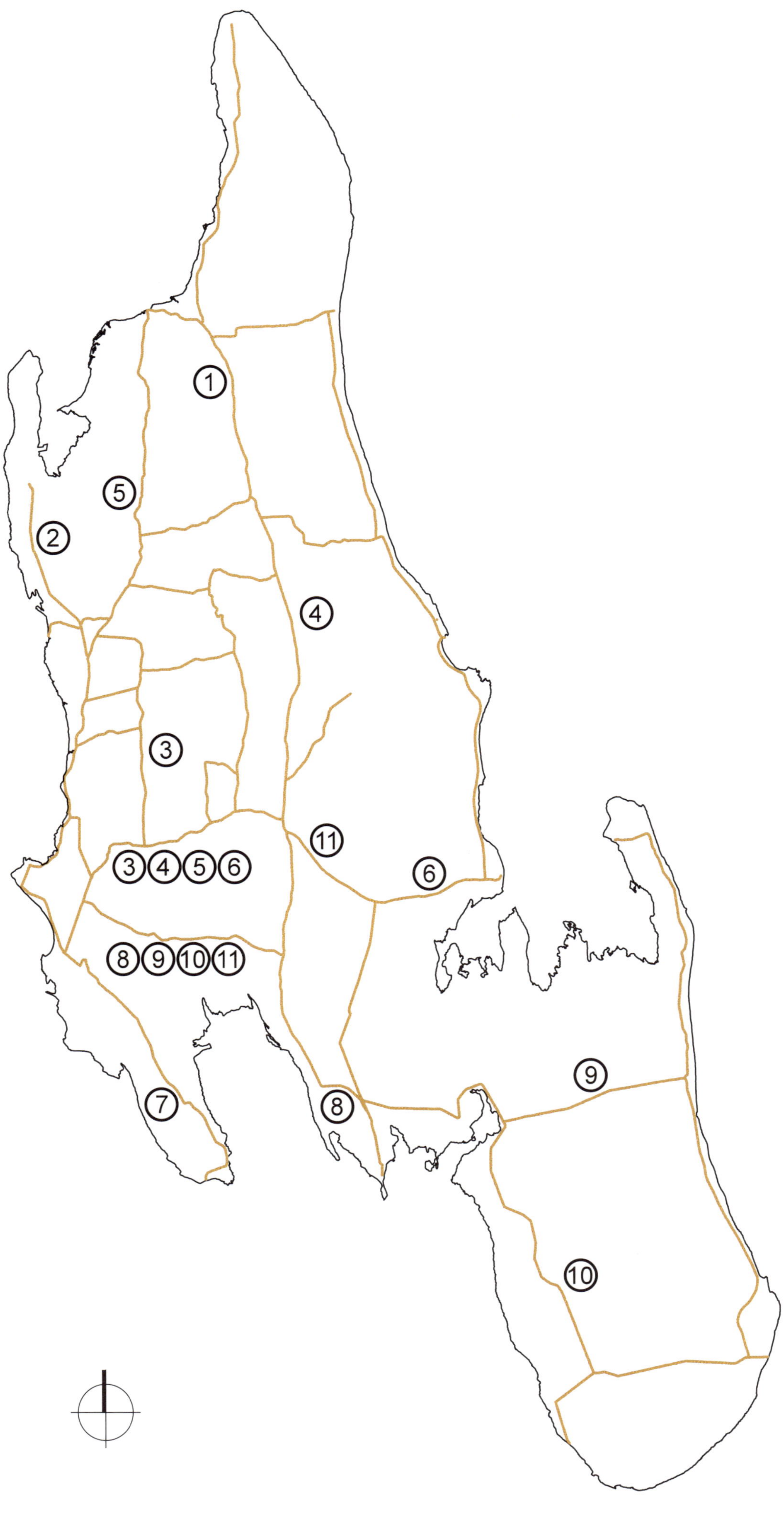

XXXI. Zanzibar Bus Routes

Sites of Special Interest

It is the entire urban fabric of Ng'ambo that gives the area its special character. Through this project it has, however, become increasingly clear that despite the general feeling of belonging and pride, an overwhelming number of people do not regard Ng'ambo as a place of historical importance and rich cultural heritage. Today there is only one listed building in the area, Livingstone House. This map identifies a number of sites of special interest that reflect the multi-layered history of Ng'ambo. While the list of identified sites is by no means exhaustive, it provides a glimpse of the cultural richness of the area as manifested in its built environment.

Ajit Singh's House (Kikwajuni Bondeni)

Ajit Singh Hoogan was a Punjab architect who moved to Zanzibar in 1937, at the age of 27. Singh worked as a draftsman at the Department of Public Works. He was responsible for some of the most prominent buildings in the city, including the Civic Centre and the Old People's Home in Sebleni. The architect's own house was built in several stages over a number of years. The design of the building reflects the African, Indian and European influences that have shaped Singh's work as an architect. It was described by one of his grandsons as having a "European exterior, an Asian interior and an African back".[39] Singh's family continues to live in the house where they now host a collection of Ajit Singh's paintings and memorabilia.

Fig 2.81: Ajit Singh's House

Bi Kidude's House (Raha Leo)

House of the famous female *taarab* singer Bi Kidude. The fame of Bi Kidude as the oldest *taarab* singer who ever lived goes well beyond the island of Zanzibar. In her house Bi Kidude often hosted music and dance events for women. The house is said to have been hidden from the gaze of men by cloths hung along the façade. Bi Kidude was also known for practicing local medicine, especially for healing asthma and treating children.

Legend

Building

Graveyard

XXXII. Sites of Special Interest

[39] Garth Andrew Myers, "Colonial Discourse and Africa's Colonized Middle: Ajit Singh's Architecture", *Historical Geography*, 27 (1995), p. 42.

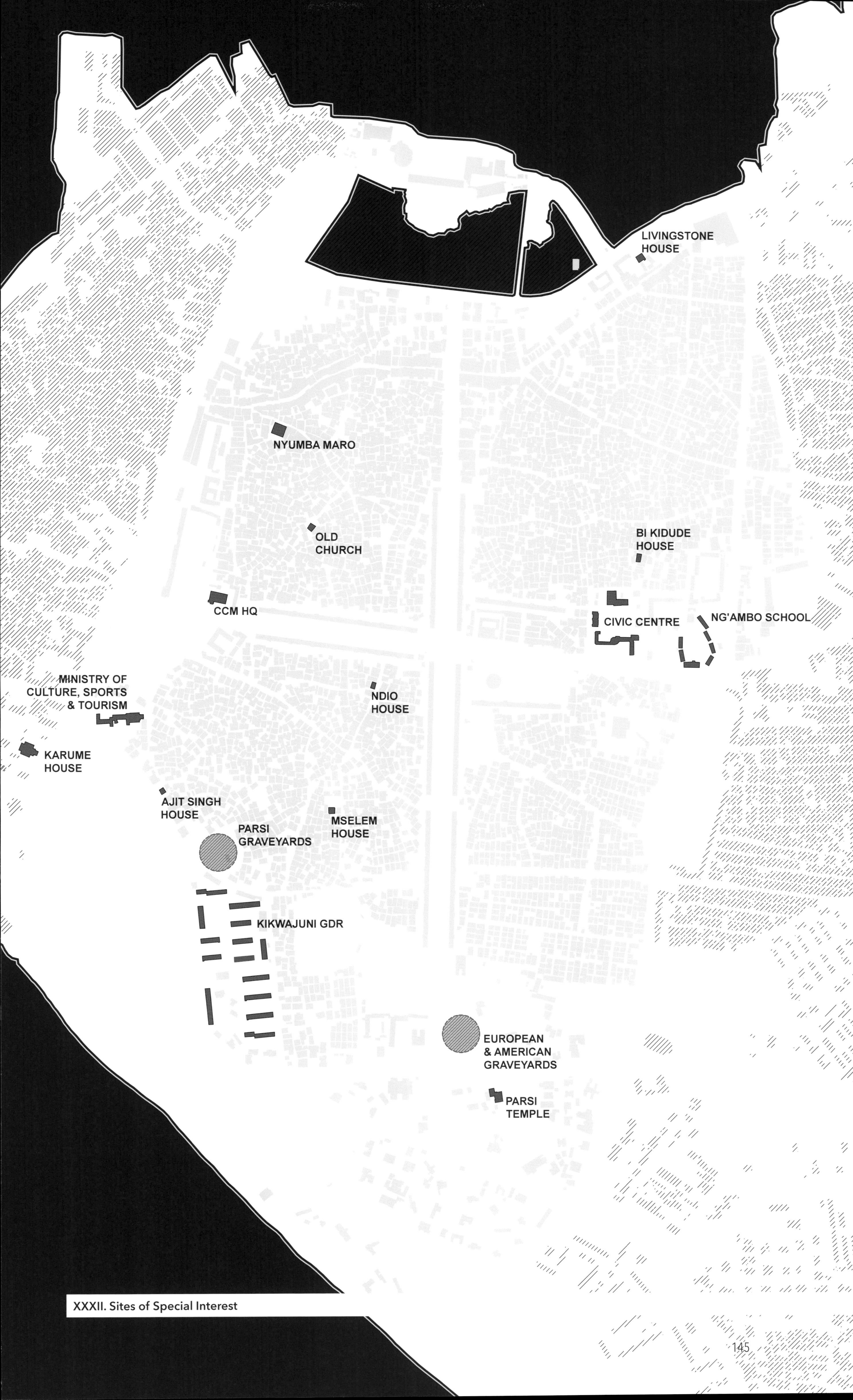

XXXII. Sites of Special Interest

CCM Headquarters (Kisiwandui)

Former headquarters of the Afro-Shirazi party, built after the revolution as a part of the Karume New Town project.

Civic Centre (Raha Leo)

The building with its surroundings was the centrepiece of the colonial post-war modernization project. Designed by Ajit Singh in 1948, it is a remarkable example of the architect's design skills and style inspired by local influences. The building originally hosted, among others, a library, community hall, the Government information officer's quarters and broadcasting facilities for Sauti ya Unguja, the 'Voice of Zanzibar'. Before the revolution the building and its surroundings were open to public, while the Civic Centre played an important part in the life of the community (for more information about the Civic Centre see Chapter 1, p. 48).

Fig 2.82: Bohora Community Graveyards

Graveyards (Miembeni & Kikwajuni)

Before 1969 it was common to bury the dead within the borders of the city. With the growth of the population and expansion of the city, many of the former burial places in Ng'ambo have been built on. The Bohora Community Graveyards in Kikwajuni and the German and English-American Cemetery are among the few that remain in place.

Fig 2.83: Karume House

Karume House (Creek Road)

The building was constructed in 1949 as a gesture of gratitude towards Sultan Khalifa, to celebrate his 70th birthday. Designed by Ajit Singh in collaboration with J.H. Sinclair, it served as an assembly hall and performance hall open to public until the revolution. After the revolution the building was taken over by TVZ and renamed Karume House. It is no longer open to public, which is regarded as a great loss by people remembering the times before the revolution.

Fig 2.84: GDR Blocks after building

Kikwajuni GDR Blocks (Kikwajuni Juu)

Modernist housing complex designed and planned by architects and planners from the GDR and built with imported building materials. The housing complex was a part of the larger New Town scheme initiated by Karume after the revolution. Construction of the Kikwajuni neighbourhood started as early as 1965 and it was the first to be completed of all the New Town projects. Although in a dilapidated condition, the neighbourhood continues to amaze with its modernist planning principles. The area is said to be known in much of the city as New Berlin Street.

Fig 2.85: Livingstone House

Livingstone House (Gulioni)

House in which the explorer David Livingstone (1813-1873) stayed before his expedition to the mainland in 1866. The house was later used by the Ismaili Community as a rest home for invalids and a location for religious meetings. Today the building hosts a small exhibition on Livingstone but is used primarily as an office building.

Ministry of Culture, Sports and Tourism (Kikwajuni Bondeni)

A building that reflects the socio-political changes that have taken place in the area. Constructed before the revolution by a local entrepreneur Sir Tayabali Karimjee as a club for the Indian community, it was renamed People's Club after the revolution and became one of the many social clubs providing entertainment for the inhabitants. After Karume's death in the 1970s the building was used as the House of Representatives. Since the early 2000s it has been the offices of the Ministry of Culture, Sports and Tourism. In architectural terms the building is an example of Tropical Modernism (*see* Fig 2.58).

Mselem House (Kikwajuni Bondeni)

Bwana Mselem was a wealthy Arab landowner and a corrupt colonial official, despised by the people of Ng'ambo for his abuse of the office for personal enrichment. Mselem was caught by his British superiors after stealing money to finance his daughter's wedding and sentenced to hard labour in the town's quarry. Siti binti Saad composed a widely popular song, still sung today, commemorating his demise (*see* Fig 1.10).

Fig 2.86: Nyumbo Maro

Ndio House (Kisiwandui)

The house in which Karume grew up and lived at the time of the revolution. The name of the house refers to the word Ndio (meaning yes) followed by the date 1962. According to urban legend this was Karume's way of expressing the inevitable end of the colonial rule and advent of the independence (*see* Fig 1.34).

Fig 2.87: Old Church

Nyumba Maro (Mtendeni)

An interesting example of caravanserai architecture, most likely built for the Shia community at the turn of the 19th century, and managed by the Wakf Commission from Stone Town. The house is located along one of the busiest streets in the area. It is a four-storey structure built around an open courtyard with a number of small flats on each floor. Travellers, widows and old people would stay in the flats for short periods of time. According to one of the tenants, the waiting list for accommodation in Nyumba Maro was very long as the flats were in high demand. The house was nationalized after the revolution. Today the building is managed by the Wakf from Stone Town.

Fig 2.88: Parsi Temple

Old Church (Vikokotoni)

The building was once reportedly used as a church. For a while it also housed the Vikokotoni Club.

Parsi Temple (Miembeni)

Until the revolution there was a large Parsi Zoroastrian community living in Zanzibar. Their former temple, surrounded by a large garden, is located in Miembeni.

3

Swahili Urbanism? Reflections and Conclusions

The first and foremost finding of the Ng'ambo Tuitakayo project is the depth and breadth of the historical riches the research unearthed, far exceeding our initial expectations. The number of maps, surveys and plans that have been drawn of Zanzibar Town and Ng'ambo over the past two centuries is exceptionally high in an African context. We have quite probably been able to collect, digitize and present the most important material in this atlas, but it is possible that many more maps, plans and surveys are still hidden away and await rediscovery.

Visual material makes up the bulk of this publication. However, it is important to mention that the accompanying text, in addition to drawing on historical sources, has been shaped by the stories and opinions of people interviewed at different stages of the project. These are comparatively few if we regard them in the light of the rich oral traditions present in the area. Nevertheless, we hope that the importance of Ng'ambo's oral history can still be felt throughout the pages.

There is little doubt that Ng'ambo, and Zanzibar Town as whole, with their rich cultural and planning histories, solicit deeper research than we have been able to carry out. Yet, we trust that the previous pages and our concluding remarks will contribute to ongoing – and inspire future – investigations of the area.

In addition (although this is beyond the scope of the present project) the uncovering of and subsequent attention paid to the rich archive material will, we hope, lead to its preservation and so assist in the protection of the historical narrative and culture of Ng'ambo.

Zanzibar Town – a Swahili City

Zanzibar Town was the largest urban settlement in East Africa for nearly one hundred years, from the 1830s to the 1920s. For a long time, as the major city of the Swahili-speaking people in East Africa, it remained the uncontested centre of the Swahili world: a role Zanzibar took over from older Swahili city states, such as Kilwa (11th-15th centuries) and Mombasa (16th-18th centuries), and lost at the beginning of the 20th century to the new East African capitals – Nairobi, Dar es Salaam and Kampala.

The origins of the modern Zanzibar Town are predominantly 19th century. Its beginnings define it as a Swahili city: a seashore settlement consisting of a repetition of freestanding Swahili houses of nearly uniform shape and size, arranged in an organic pattern and organised around two major functions. Commercial activities centred on the port (the original fishing settlement or *diko*) and the custom house; social activities centred on public and elite private buildings, such as mosques, madrassas, administration buildings, and the town palaces of rich merchants and rulers.

Due to the typically cosmopolitan nature of coastal Swahili cities, buildings that make up the urban tissue tend to absorb foreign architectural influences to a significant degree. In Zanzibar, the main foreign influences came from Oman during the first part of the 19th century, and were later superseded by Indian and British influences from around the 1880s. International and global architectural influences, in particular modernism, reached Zanzibar during the 1960s and continue to have an impact today.

The loose Swahili urban tissue in Zanzibar Town densified over time. During the modernization à la Swahili, single-storied Swahili houses gradually started to be replaced by multi-storied stone buildings. These buildings often enlarged their footprint and began to form continuous street fronts and urban blocks. The process started in Stone Town, but parts of Ng'ambo developed in a similar fashion at the beginning of the 20th century and continue to do so today.

Ng'ambo, as defined in this atlas, was to a large degree built up by the 1920s. The urban tissue - with roads, squares and recreation grounds as we know them today - was largely present by that date. In a morphological sense, Ng'ambo and Stone Town have the same roots with Stone Town taking the lead in the process of densification and modernization. With regard to the social and cultural aspects, Ng'ambo and Stone Town started to part ways at the end of the 19th century. The racial segregation that was introduced and formalized under the British Protectorate caused the purely geographical division formed by the creek to become a socio-economic and ethnic separation as well - demarcating Ng'ambo as a 'native quarter' and reserving Stone Town for the foreign elites.

Segregation changed the internal dynamic between the parts of the city, from closely connected and interdependent to what, from an outsider's perspective, could seem like a city of two worlds. This image was further strengthened by the urban conservation initiatives started in the 1990s, and the declaration of Stone Town as a World Heritage Site in 2000. On the one hand, these interventions drew attention to Stone Town, creating new opportunities and encouraging tourism to the coastal Swahili city; but on the other, they reaffirmed the intangible division between Stone Town (old and of architectural, cultural and historical merit) and Ng'ambo (new and of no architectural, cultural or historical merit).

Fig 3.1: Fishermen mending their nets at Mnazi Mmoja

Spontaneous Urban and Architectural Development of Ng'ambo

During our research we found Ng'ambo's typological and morphological changes over time remarkably consistent. The redevelopment, or modernization of Ng'ambo has been a continuous process since the 'completion' of the urbanization in the 1920s. It can be argued that city's built environment is gradually transforming on two levels. One is the micro-level of the individual residential units, the other is the macro-level related to the overall changing image of the city.

The first level of urban transformation can be regarded as a continuation of what Myers credits to the 'custom of perfectionism', visible on the individual and private scale and starting with a piecemeal rehabilitation of dwellings by replacing perishable with more durable materials. The second level is a result of broader economic and cultural transformations manifested, among others, in the emergence of new building typologies across the area.

For the individual homeowners, the overall transformation of the physical landscape of the city may matter less on a daily basis than the gradual transformations of the single-storey Swahili houses in their immediate neighbourhoods. In the case of more affluent owners, upgrading and modernization of residential units can include introduction of new building typologies such as multi-storey Swahili or Swahili 2020. However, for the majority of people transformation will take the form of gradual, structural or aesthetic improvements and changes to single-storey Swahili houses conducted according to their means.

There is a general tendency among homeowners to replace coral-and-lime constructions with cement-block constructions. The 'custom of perfectionism' is manifested in constant improvements of the condition of buildings, but it can also be seen in the enrichment of the façades, serving to indicate the wealth and status of the owner - rather like the wooden doors found in Stone Town. The more exuberant the façade, the more likely it is that there is an affluent owner behind its doors. Decorative elements are used with quite some liberty in Ng'ambo. However, they appear to be coming in waves and follow clear fashions whose sources can be found either in the architecture of Stone Town or beyond the borders of the island. While it might be difficult to establish a clear pattern, the decorative elements appear to be spreading across the neighbourhoods on a 'borrowing ideas from the next-door neighbour' basis, which often results in clusters of buildings with similar arrangements of the available decorative repertoire.

The ongoing process of modernization and improvement of residential units manifested through the exchange of perishable building materials for more permanent ones has a long history in the context of single-storey Swahili houses in the area. According to our findings, there appears to be little correlation between the building technology and the building condition in respective structures, even though buildings in good condition are more likely to be constructed of cement blocks or with a concrete frame. This, according to our observations, has more to do with the date of the construction of the building than the building technology applied as such.

When compared with the findings of the field work conducted by Garth Myers in 1992, it appears that the overall distribution of buildings in good and poor condition across Ng'ambo follows the socio-spatial hierarchy present in the area since the late 19th century. The north-western parts of Ng'ambo, located closer to Stone Town, have generally been more affluent than the remaining parts. In the physical realm this translates into the declining condition and scanter decoration of buildings moving eastward, a tendency also visible in the area today.

A next step in privately initiated redevelopment in Ng'ambo is the complete replacement of the Swahili house by a multi-storey building. There is no alternative other than to rebuild the building from scratch, since it is technically impossible to extend a traditional single-storey Swahili house vertically. We have noted a persisting rationale behind the typological development of residential units, expressing itself in the change from single-storey to multi-storey buildings based on the original footprint of the Swahili house. While not able to verify the information, we suspect that the interior arrangement (standard floor plan with rows of rooms on a central corridor) is likely to be repeated on the upper floor levels of multi-storey Swahili or Swahili 2020 buildings appearing in the area.

The earliest examples of multi-storied developments can be found on the outskirts of Ng'ambo, in particular on the northern edges along Malawi (previously Hollis) Road. Our research also revealed a relation between the location of new investment and car access. New multi-storey buildings can usually be found next to thoroughfares and roads that are navigable by motor vehicles and not solely by foot, as is the majority of Ng'ambo's densely built urban tissue.

The bottom-up redevelopment process was controlled during the colonial years by the authorities, but was much less monitored after the revolution. The lack of control resulted in a general tendency to extend the footprint of houses during redevelopment. This is gradually leading to an encroachment of private buildings on open spaces and secondary roads. At the same time, the streetscape in Ng'ambo has deteriorated considerably over the past fifty years. Subsequent authorities have for a long time neglected the public realm, and this has resulted in deterioration of pavements, drainage, street lighting and other infrastructure. In addition, the loss of trees – socially, culturally and historically important for the area, being valued for their healing, spiritual, and economic properties as well as for providing shade from the bright sun – is evident (*see* Chapter 2, pp. 110-112 and 126).

Planned Urban and Architectural Development of Ng'ambo

In general, it can be stated that Ng'ambo, notwithstanding neglect, continued to develop in its own, organic way throughout the 19th and first half of the 20th centuries. Planned interventions took place only at the periphery, following proposals by Lanchester (1923), and by town planners working for the colonial administration.

It was only from the 1940s onwards, that the authorities made substantial moves to redevelop Ng'ambo. The most visible remains of these interventions are the Civic Centre in Raha Leo, Mapembeani, and the orthogonally laid out residential neighbourhoods of social housing in Gulioni, Mwembetanga and Miembeni. Miembeni, laid out in the 1950s on plans drawn by Geoffrey Mills, is particularly notable as it stands out besides other neighbourhoods as typologically nearly uniform. It has maintained its original grid pattern until the present and nearly all the buildings are single storey, a condition we believe to be related to the fact that Miembeni is geographically removed from areas of intensified commercial activity.

Although considerable investments were made by the erstwhile colonial administration to redevelop the 'native quarters', they did not shake Ng'ambo on its foundations in the same way the revolution did. Until the end, the plans of colonial officers continued to be drafted with the Swahili house as the basic grain of the urban tissue, though now laid out in an orderly instead of an organic pattern. The plans of Karume broke away from this tradition completely. Karume's New Town project envisioned the complete replacement of Zanzibar Town by a modernist city. Michenzani, at the centre of Ng'ambo, was selected for the first stage of this unique (in the context of post-independence Africa) rebuilding scheme.

New Towns are, as a rule, built on greenfield locations unless an historical city is destroyed by acts of war or nature – such as Noto in Sicily, destroyed by an earthquake, or Rotterdam in the Netherlands, bombarded in World War II. To replace a thriving historical city, or a larger part of it, by completely new urban tissue is a rarity. The incomplete, yet drastic, rebuilding of Ng'ambo by Karume marked the end of large-scale urban redevelopment projects in the area. From the 1970s (when the New Town project largely came to a halt) to the end of the 20th century, little to no government or private investment was made in this part of the city. One more attempt to redevelop Ng'ambo was made in the 1982 Chang-Kequan masterplan, proposing a CBD around the areas of Kijagwani, Mitiulaya and Miembeni. The plan was not implemented, except for the construction of the Post Office at Kijagwani and ZECO office at Mitiulaya.

Private investments that visibly altered the urban fabric of the area, started to gain momentum only by the beginning of the 21st century. This is also the case with government projects, which have – so far – been focused primarily on single architectural projects such as the completion of the Michenzani blocks, the Public Library or the Uhuru Tower.

Fig 3.2: The changing face of Ng'ambo

Fig 3.3: Symbolic developments

Ng'ambo Today and Tomorrow

Ng'ambo's landscape is predominantly low-rise, but a steady upward growth spearheaded by new investments is gradually transforming its skyline. Over the years, the area has become a multi-layered patchwork of typologies, styles and building technologies, with a mix of elements witnessing various moments in its history. While Ng'ambo maintains its predominantly residential character, new service and commercial districts are emerging along main thoroughfares such as Mlandege Road, Creek Road and Malawi Road - indicating that the decades-long building impasse has come to an end.

The urban fabric of Ng'ambo is dominated by two tissues: the organic Swahili and the modernist Karume New Town. Their juxtaposition, in architectural and spatial terms, is a unique characteristic of the place. It is also a reminder of a turbulent episode in Zanzibar's history, a symbol of the incomplete modernist project of nation building, and an example of two drastically different frames for everyday life.

Recently, the place of Karume's unfulfilled holistic vision for the city has been taken by the aspirations of individual investors and dreams of inhabitants, to whom cities like Abu Dhabi and Seoul have become the example to imitate. Changes in the city are dynamic, but alongside the architectural/urban push for (post)modernity and global language, Ng'ambo's past can still be felt in its urban landscape. The elusive division between the two parts of the city continues to linger over the place and it is still commonly believed that Stone Town is the 'cultural and historic heart' of Zanzibar's capital (as if to confirm this notion there is only one listed building in Ng'ambo - Livingstone House). Adopting such initiatives as UNESCO's Historic Urban Landscape recommendations in the research and drafting of a local area plan for Ng'ambo is one of the first steps towards reviving the old connection between the two parts of the city. It is also the first effort by the authorities to officially acknowledge the historic importance of neighbourhoods that have for years been key in shaping the identity of the Zanzibar Town we know today. Over the years Ng'ambo has been an important setting for cultural and political activities, filled with venues for sports, music and dance that provided opportunity for people living on both sides of the creek to interact. Furthermore, there are numerous sites of historic interest in the area that, above all, testify to the active part Ng'ambo has played in the subsequent development of the city.

Through our project it has become clear to us that the richness and complexity of the urban culture that has shaped Zanzibar Town and grown out of the connection between Stone Town and Ng'ambo is not a matter of the past. It continues to be manifested in place names, architecture, urban tissue, in memory, and above all in the way the inhabitants reinvent themselves on a daily basis. Principles of Swahili urbanism seem to be deeply engrained in the contemporary city and are a defining part of the resilience of Zanzibar's rich culture. This certainly raises the question about the unique qualities of the processes that have shaped Zanzibar Town, in the context of other cities sharing common Swahili roots. But it also suggests the possibility of considering Swahili Urbanism, often regarded as a matter of historic research, as a living concept and not only a subject of the past.

Fig 3.4: Ng'ambo today and tomorrow

4

Project History and Context

Ng'ambo Tuitakayo was initiated in 2012 by the Department of Urban and Rural Planning (DoURP) in Zanzibar, UNESCO and African Architecture Matters, with a pilot project on the mapping of the historic environment of Ng'ambo supported by the UNESCO Dar es Salaam office, the Netherlands-Fund-in-Trust and the Zanzibar Social Security Fund. In this first phase, a small triangle was mapped to sample the availability of sources, documenting the richness of Ng'ambo's history, cultural and urban fabric. The project grew to become a collaborative project between the DoURP, the Municipality of Amsterdam and AAMatters (*see* Chapter 1, pp. 78-83).

It is the aim of Ng'ambo Tuitakayo to create planning policies that are firmly grounded in the notion of heritage-based urban development for the future city centre of Zanzibar Town, and to increase awareness in Zanzibar of the value of local culture and heritage in development, influenced by the new approach underpinned in the UNESCO Recommendation on Historic Urban Landscape. The project resulted in a draft of *Planning Policy Guidelines for Historic Urban Areas* (2014), *Zanzibar Town City Centre Local Area Plan* (2016) and *Ng'ambo Atlas: Historic Urban Landscape of Zanzibar Town's 'Other Side'* (2018).

An holistic approach to urban planning acknowledging the dynamic and evolving nature of the city has been at the heart of planning actions undertaken by DoURP since its foundation in 2011. The Government of Zanzibar has shown its ambition to develop solutions for the inherent challenge of planning for the future, while keeping alive the past by joining UNESCO in the development of the Historic Urban Landscape (HUL) approach. It was proactive in attracting UNESCO to Zanzibar in December 2009 and August 2011 for two workshops that would, as part of a process also involving other towns along the Swahili coast, contribute to the development of the HUL Recommendation adopted by the UNESCO member states on 10 November 2011.

Subsequently, the Government of Zanzibar took its ambitions further by adopting the HUL approach for the integration of development, conservation and quality of life in Zanzibar through spatial planning. HUL played a central role in the *National Spatial Development Strategy* (NSDS) of 2014, integrating the development of historical urban areas with the overall strategy. This NSDS has served as a guideline for all subsequently produced local area plans on the islands.

The material presented in this publication, as well as the overall methodology applied in the project process, are results of the commitment by the Government of Zanzibar to test the HUL recommendations in an African context.[40]

[40] For further information on Zanzibar's involvement in development of the HUL recommendations, see Ron van Oers (ed.), *Report on the Historic Urban Landscape Workshops and Field Activities on the Swahili Coast in East Africa 2011-2012*, (Paris, France, UNESCO World Heritage Centre, 2013).

Fig 4.1: Ng'ambo Tuitakayo
Workshop, 2014.

Ng'ambo Tuitakayo: Collaboration Between Zanzibar and Amsterdam

This cooperation began in 2014, as part of the abovementioned pilot project focusing on the historical *mitaa* (neighbourhoods) of Kisiwandui, Kisimamajongoo and Michenzani located in the buffer zone of the World Heritage Site. It started by contributing to the extensive mapping and survey process and concluded with a visioning event called *Ng'ambo tuitakayo!* 'Ng'ambo as we want it!'. The aim of this event was to capture inhabitants' visions for the future of the project area. Findings of the pilot informed the subsequent phase of the project, which entailed the 13 *shehias* and parts of the Malindi *shehia* lying within the borders of the future city centre.

The government of Zanzibar and the City of Amsterdam are both custodians of a UNESCO World Heritage Site, albeit in differing cultural, economic and geographical contexts. The common membership in the community of UNESCO World Heritage Site administrators brings a number of shared responsibilities and poses shared challenges concerned with the management of the sites and the development of the surrounding areas. While each of the cities has its own challenges, the common denominator has enabled a mutual exchange of knowledge throughout the process that has benefitted both parts.

Ng'ambo Tuitakayo was set up in a research-by-planning and planning-by-research fashion, and can be regarded as both experimental and innovative in the context of Zanzibar. The project sought to apply a holistic approach to urban planning in which sociological and historical research methods were combined with planning, architectural and urban design methods. At the same time as conducting extensive research and field surveys, work on the local area plan was being developed. Findings of the research provided a basis for the development of the LAP, while the work on the LAP raised questions that the field survey would follow up on. It soon became clear that the material collected should not just serve the LAP, but needed to be made public for further use by scholars and planners alike – hence this publication.

Fig 4.2: Ng'ambo Tuitakayo
Visit from Amsterdam to Zanzibar, 2014.

Fig 4.3: Ng'ambo Tuitakayo
Visit from Zanzibar to Amsterdam, 2014.

Studios and expert consultations taking place in October 2015 resulted in the first draft of the Ng'ambo LAP. In January 2016, a symposium was organized in Amsterdam to consult external experts on (in)tangible cultural heritage mapping. The second draft of the document was in place in January 2016. Between March and May 2016, stakeholders and community consultations presenting preliminary plans were held in the area. The final draft of the LAP as well as the maps for *Ng'ambo Atlas: Historic Urban Landscape of Zanzibar Town's 'Other Side'* (2018) were exhibited and discussed with the community and stakeholders in June 2016. Preliminary outcomes and findings of Ng'ambo Tuitakayo were also presented to the UNESCO HUL network, for which Ng'ambo serves as a pilot for implementation of HUL recommendations in East Africa. On 13 May 2017, the Government of Zanzibar, under the leadership of the President of Zanzibar, officially approved the *Zanzibar Town City Centre Local Area Plan* as a development plan for the Zanzibar Town City Centre for the next ten years.

Fig 4.4: Finding Stories
Symposium in Amsterdam, 2016.

Fig 4.5: Ng'ambo Tuitakayo
Project presentation, 2016.

Fig 4.6: Ng'ambo Tuitakayo
Project presentation, 2016.

UNESCO Historic Urban Landscape Approach Applied to the Project

"The urban area understood as the result of a historic layering of cultural and natural values and attributes, extending beyond the notion of 'historic centre' or 'ensemble' to include the broader urban context and its geographical setting. This wider context includes notably the site's topography, geomorphology, hydrology and natural features, its built environment, both historic and contemporary, its infrastructures above and below ground, its open spaces and gardens, its land use patterns and spatial organization, perceptions and visual relationships, as well as all other elements of the urban structure. It also includes social and cultural practices and values, economic processes and the intangible dimensions of heritage as related to diversity and identity".[41]

This holistic approach to urban conservation means a shift for planners and their processes. Mapping and research are key to an increased understanding of not only the present-day physical fabric of a city, but the multiple layers and facets of natural and cultural, tangible and intangible heritage, together with contemporary expressions and future needs and aspirations. People and their lives, the value of culture, matter in conservation and planning. The HUL approach also emphasizes the connection between the city's (historic) core and its periphery, as well as connectivity in time and space beyond the city boundaries.

The tools offered are many. HUL has collected, and continues to advance, best practices and experience the world over. The toolkit emphasizes four key areas: civic engagement, knowledge and planning, regulatory systems, and financial tools.[42]

The following steps, as suggested in the introduction to the UNESCO HUL Recommendation, formed a road-map for the Ng'ambo Tuitakayo project.[43] They serve as a reference by which the application of the HUL approach in the context of Ng'ambo can be assessed at each moment in the process. It should, however, be noted that implementation of the HUL approach in the area is an ongoing and evolving process.

1. To undertake comprehensive surveys and mapping of the historic cities' natural, cultural and human resources.

2. To reach consensus using participatory planning and stakeholder consultations on what values to protect for transmission to future generations, and to determine the attributes that bear these values.

3. To assess the vulnerability of such attributes to socio-economic pressures and the impacts of climate change.

4. To integrate urban heritage values and their vulnerability status into a wider framework of city development, which will provide indications of areas of heritage sensitivity that require careful attention to planning, design and implementation of development projects.

5. To prioritize actions for conservation and development.

6. To establish the appropriate partnerships and local management frameworks for each of the projects identified for conservation and development, as well as to develop mechanisms for the coordination of the various activities between different actors, both public and private.

[41] UNESCO, *Recommendation on the Historic Urban Landscape*. Adopted by the General Conference at its 36th session, 10 November 2011, Paris.

[42] Ibid.

[43] Ibid.

A key objective of the application of the HUL approach in Zanzibar has been to build a framework for ensuring sustainable change in parts of the city subjected to rapid urban development, and to encourage a revision of the existing perceptions of heritage values. DoURP, together with AAMatters and UNESCO, therefore organised an international conference to integrate expertise and experiences from other places where HUL was applied. The conference on 11-13 February 2014 was integrated with a stakeholder workshop to enable experts and local stakeholders to meet and exchange views directly. This resulted in a set of recommendations for the future work on Ng'ambo.

In practice, application of the HUL required an adjustment of the recommendations to the local context and scope of the project. Ng'ambo Tuitakayo provides a model for future planning activities in Zanzibar based on a people-centred approach, partnerships, and collaboration with local stakeholders. It has also encouraged a better understanding of social and cultural values of Zanzibar Town among the local authorities and community. Mapping of Ng'ambo's cultural resources enabled the identification of areas of heritage sensitivity and an assessment of their vulnerability. The documentation produced as a result of the project is available for future reference. The knowledge database created through the process testifies to the rich history of the place and is currently being made available through OSM and Wikipedia.

Fig 4.7: Ng'ambo Tuitakayo
Workshop, 2014.

Fig 4.8: Ng'ambo Tuitakayo
Workshop, 2014.

5

Project Methodology

The following section presents information on the methodology applied in the research and mapping of Ng'ambo which served to identify the historical and contemporary cultural assets of the area. The process was shaped by its purpose-oriented aim to apply the HUL approach in planning work. The historic urban landscape research was conducted in two phases over a period of eight months. It consisted of a survey of the built environment (as a key element of the tangible heritage) and mapping of the immaterial culture (as part of the intangible heritage) and took place between October 2015 and April 2016. Simultaneously with this field work, a literature review and desktop research were conducted, which informed the overall process of collecting data. Survey information gathered throughout the project including visual documentation of the built environment was stored in the Zanzibar Land Information System (ZALIS). Mapping results were also published on the Open Street Map in order to encourage a greater transparency of the governmental processes and enable a more integrated top-down and bottom-up data collection in the future. This publication as well as the process through which the materials presented in the atlas were collected can be regarded as an outcome of the application of HUL recommendations in practice.

Creating a Starting Point for the Field Survey

The creation of the 2015 base map presented in the LAP and used during the field survey is a combination of three different components:

1. Latest CAD drawing of Zanzibar Town (DoURP, ca.2007)

2. Open Street Map (OSM) building polygons

3. Drone-generated aerial image of Zanzibar Town city centre (World Bank, October 2015)

The CAD drawing of the DoURP (1), although providing outdated information, was the most accurate drawing existing at the time. In an effort to create an updated 2015 base map, it was decided to keep this drawing as a main reference, merging it with the most recent information from other sources.

An exported database from OSM (2) containing building polygons was projected over the DoURP CAD drawing (1), in order to bring the files up to date.

The OSM polygons were all created by the Ng'ambo Tuitakayo ground-mapping team during the digitization of the hand-generated field maps, using the aerial image (3) as a reference. This aerial image is assembled from a series of photos taken from a drone flying above Zanzibar Town city centre in October 2015.

It should be noted that the aerial image (3) and OSM polygons (2), although carrying the most recent information, are not as accurate as a professional, on site, topographic survey can be. The newest building outlines were created by visual observation and a fault margin of up to two metres should be reckoned with.

Desktop Mapping

In order to gain an in-depth understanding of the historic development of the project area, desktop mapping was carried out. The task was conducted in two phases. The first phase took place in advance of field mapping and comprised extensive archival research into the National Archives of Zanzibar, Survey Department Archives and Planning Department Archives in the DoURP. The collected material was analysed and processed in the second phase. This resulted in a selection of relevant maps, surveys and plans which inform the historical aspect of the project. The selected maps were georeferenced in order to provide a better understanding of the urban genesis and development of Ng'ambo. The second phase was carried out simultaneously with the field mapping, thus allowing both parts to be continuously informed by the findings of the other. Maps and surveys retrieved from DoURP were scanned and stored in ZALIS database.

The desktop inventory in the second stage of the project continued to build on the information collected during the first stage. Findings from the desktop inventory were arranged into a matrix, which served as a reference for the field work and was continuously updated.

Survey of the Building Stock: Objectives and Approach

The survey of the built environment covered 13 *shehias* located within the borders of the future city centre, and parts of the Malindi *shehia* and consisted of approximately 5,000 objects (*see* Chapter 1, p. 74). It was based on the external appearance of the buildings. The main goal of the survey was to provide an up-to-date image of the character and condition of the existing building stock. To this end an inventory of each building based on the categories typology, style, condition, building technique and roof structure was made. Findings of the survey were translated into five maps representing the respective categories. They also served to identify emerging trends in Ng'ambo's built environment and in distinguishing its specific urban characteristics, which were later incorporated into the LAP.

Phase I: Area exploration and preparation

The team conducted two exploratory walks through the project area in order to gain an overview of the existing urban tissue. The exploratory walks were followed by a typology workshop where a document with urban and architectural typologies as well as other important values for the inventory process was drafted.

Phase II: Inventory

Following the topography of the area, Ng'ambo was divided into four quadrants formed by the Michenzani blocks. Each section was mapped by at least one group. Groups varied in size from two to three people. The inventory was carried out based on the external appearance of the existing structures, using a mapping sheet with various values, the area base map, and photographic documentation. The field work was followed up by briefings where observations were shared in order to continuously improve the methodology and clarify uncertainties regarding classifications of structures.

Phase III: Data transfer

Transfer of the collected data into the Open Street Map system was an ongoing process. In order to minimize the margin of error and secure the quality of collected data, findings from the field work were crosschecked with the photographic documentation before being transferred into the OSM system.

Fig 5.1: Phase 1: Area exploration and preparation

Fig 5.2: Phase 2: Inventory

Fig 5.3: Phase 3: Data transfer

Mapping of the Intangible Culture: Objectives and Approach

During the second phase of the project a team consisting of members of the DoURP, AAMatters and a community liaison representative conducted mapping of the immaterial culture. Due to time constrains, the mapping included only 11 of the *shehias* that made up the plan area. The mapping resulted in nine working-maps and five maps showing selected data from the research, arranged in the following categories: Toponymy, Places for Cultural Activities, Public Recreation, Places for Social Interaction, Handcrafts.

The goal of the intangible culture heritage mapping was to record the (immaterial) history within the physical realm. The collected data are not restricted to any particular period in time and include both contemporary and historical information.

As a starting point for the mapping, the project adopted the notion of 'storyscapes'. The objective was to encourage individuals from Ng'ambo to identify important communal, cultural and historical places through their own stories. Mapping took form of walks with informants across respective neighbourhoods, during which informants identified places they considered of significance. These walks also served to collect social and historical data *in situ*. Interviews conducted *in situ* draw on both experiential and abstract forms of knowledge and enabled a construction of a more interactive picture of the area, while the walks, in general, were found to provide a relaxed and beneficial context for collecting data.

Interviews conducted during the project were both formal and informal. Informants ('storytellers') included both women and men and were usually identified on an ongoing basis by the prime contact in the field, the *shehia* (the leader of the respective administrative unit) or by other inhabitants. Hence, the success of the mapping process depended to a large extent on the collaboration of the local inhabitants. The majority of the interviewees belonged to what could be considered as the 'older generation' of inhabitants of Ng'ambo, born before or around the revolution. This age bias is a result of the overall research focus on historic aspects related to the area. Consequently the majority of formal interviews were conducted with the men and women of an older generation. The nature of the interviews varied from in-depth interviews covering a wide array of questions to more informal conversations with chance encounters. Discussions with members of the younger generation of Ng'ambo usually resulted from chance meetings in the field. In addition, a number of interviews on the general history of the Zanzibar Town were conducted with informants identified as experts, due to their professional background providing an extra layer to the understanding of the history and culture of Ng'ambo.

Mapping of the intangible cultural heritage was guided by the practically oriented nature of the task. With this in mind, a number of pre-defined themes were developed to provide a framework for the interviews and field research. Guiding themes for the mapping were identified through desktop research and a literature review. Nevertheless, the course of the day-to-day field research and the nature of the information collected was above all defined by people encountered in the field.

Phase I: Field mapping

Field work was conducted over a period of approximately 30 days covering 11 *shehias* in Ng'ambo.

The team interviewed between one and three informants from each *shehia*. Informal walks around the area were conducted with one of the informants. A map with annotations describing each of the mapped elements was produced based on the information gathered during the informal walk. Information presented in the maps was followed up by photographic documentation enabling identification of the setting of the story or the element referred to by the informant.

In total, the team conducted 41 interviews. The interviews were either recorded or filmed, depending on the preferences of the informant. Some of the storytellers were consulted more than once. Each of the interviews has been transcribed. Selected walks through the area were recorded on camera. The data collected through the mapping and the documentation of the field work has been stored in the ZALIS database.

Fig 5.4: Phase 1: Field mapping

Fig 5.5: Phase 1: Field mapping

Phase II: Data analysis

The collected data and information extracted from the interviews was organised into a framework which served as a roadmap during the field research. Continuously updated, it later became a tool for creating an overview of the collected data. Overall, nine maps covering various aspects of the 11 *shehias* were produced. After completing the field work, researchers analysed the collected data on the basis of the framework and findings covered in the field maps. In the end five maps, representing categories covering a wide range of findings from the research, were produced. The final analysis and description of findings is based on the information represented in these maps. A number of recommendations for the LAP based on the overall findings of the field work were made.

Use of Open Sources

Tools used in the mapping process apply the open data concept, which supports the idea that certain kinds of data (such as geo-data) should be open and freely available. The following open-source tools were used in the mapping of the building stock: Open Street Map: a free and editable web world map, created entirely by volunteering contributors; JOSM: one of the available Open Street Map editors; QGIS: free and open-source geographic information system (GIS) software, created, maintained and developed by volunteers; Wiki: user-editable pages and sites that provide a possibility for collaborative shaping of the content and structure of the page.

In order to transfer the collected information to the OSM-system, each new classification or feature defined by the NGT team had to be described and presented for approval to the Wiki community. As a parallel process, a number of Wikipedia pages were launched to define the classifications and features introduced by the team to the OSM.

Glossary and Definition of Terms

Baraza:
covered reception area in front of a house
Origin: Swahili

Godown:
storage shed
Origin: Indonesian

Cordon sanitaire:
green strip between districts to keep population groups separate
Origin: French

Mabati:
corrugated metal roof sheet
Origin: Swahili

Maskan / pl. maskani:
meeting place for men
Origin: Arabic

Dala dala:
public transport in Tanzania: usually a minibus carrying about 15 passengers
Origin: Swahili

Makuti:
roofing made of tiles of woven palm leaves
Origin: Swahili

Dhow:
freight vessel
Origin: Arabic, Swahili

Mtaa / pl. mitaa:
neighbourhood or town ward
Origin: Swahili

Ua:
courtyard
Origin: Swahili

Duka:
shop
Origin: Indian

Wakf:
Muslim institution that manages the legacies and donations of the faithful, often in the form of property
Origin: Arabic

Building typologies:

Apartment building: a multi-storey residential building. In contrast to Swahili 2020 buildings, apartment blocks are not built on the footprint of a single-storey Swahili house. The typology is distinguished on the basis of the function of the buildings, not their architectural or urban form. The term is therefore applied widely and encompasses all purpose-built structures housing multiple families, unless indicated otherwise.

Government: a typology developed on the basis of the function of the building not its form. It is used to classify buildings which are (currently) in use by the government.

High Street: a term describing mixed-use and service buildings located in the vicinity of areas identified as commercial high streets. The typology is developed on the basis of the function of the building as well as the context in which it is located. As a type of building it is a relatively recent addition to the urban landscape of Zanzibar Town, corresponding with the gradual modernization of the commercial sectors in the city. There are certain recurring architectural elements that are associated with this building typology such as the visual emphasis on street elevation and extensive use of glazing. The name is derived from the British urban typology.

Indian shopfront: a term describing mixed-use, two-storied buildings usually located along narrow commercial roads, creating rows of houses. Built on a narrow footprint, the Indian shopfront has commercial space located on the ground floor and residential quarters on the first level. The typology is traditionally found both in Stone Town and Ng'ambo.

Madrasa: refers to a specific type of religious school or college for the study of Islam.

Market stall: a typology developed on the basis of function, describing a detached one-storey structure built for commercial purposes.

Modern Indian shopfront: a typology derived from the Indian shopfront, describing structures with commercial space on the ground floor. In contrast with the traditional Indian shopfront, this typology has more than one residential level.

Multi-storey Swahili: a term describing a building typology of usually two-storey buildings, built on the footprint of a single-storey Swahili house.

Others: a category encompassing all non-conforming residential, leisure, public, educational and functional buildings.

Single-storey Swahili: a term describing the building typology of single-storey houses found in Ng'ambo. The typology is developed on the basis of the analogy between the form and function (primary function residential, secondary function commercial) of the building. Customarily a rectangular, one-storey house with three to six rooms arranged around an axial corridor, with outbuildings comprising kitchen and toilet located at the back and separated by a small courtyard from the living area.

Swahili 2020: a term describing contemporary multi-storey buildings built on one or multiple footprints of an old Swahili house. The typology is developed on the basis of the analogy between the form and function (primary function residential, secondary function commercial) of the building. It is characterized by high ground floors and vertical expansion of the envelope.

Suburban villa: a term describing detached family houses surrounded by a wall or a garden. The suburban villa is mostly found on the edges of the city. Buildings conforming to this typology can also be found in the inner city, usually built with little or no consideration to the surrounding urban tissue.

Building styles:

Art Deco: a stylistic term defined by geometrical ornamentation, bold use of colours and stylized decoration. Prevalent in Zanzibar Town is an Indian-inspired Art Deco style. Applied to single-storey Swahili houses in a simplified manner through use of individual decorative elements associated with Art Deco on the front elevation.

British Colonial: a broad stylistic term applied to buildings built in the British Imperial style and / or with reference to the Saracenic influences introduced to the island by J.H. Sinclair. Defined by eclectic use of classicist, orientalist and gothic elements and Mangalore tiled roofs.

Classic Swahili: a style of a Swahili house in its most basic form without any additional decorative elements.

Postmodern: a term describing buildings which use decorative elements often, but not exclusively, borrowed from historical styles. The term is applied broadly and can be used to describe the style of buildings where the use of decorative elements is consistent throughout the elevations, as well as buildings with mixed application of multiple historical citations (i.e. the use of crenulations, columns or pilasters as decorative elements in one building).

Modernism: a stylistic term applied both to structures which are thoroughly modernist in their concept, structure and appearance (e.g. Bwawani Complex, Michenzani Blocks) and to describe the stylistic appearance of Swahili houses mainly defined by projecting horizontal slabs over the entrance, projecting geometrical sunshades over windows and the characteristic, and widely used in the 1970s, two-leveled split roof.

Hypermodern: a term applied to the stylistic appearance of buildings that are not particularly sensitive to the environment and are characterized by mixed use of materials, most often including glazing. Example: Uhuru Tower. (For further discussion of the hypermodern style in the African context see A.S. Folkers, *Modern Architecture in Africa*).

Indian-influenced: a style derived from Indian architecture, characterized by intricate woodwork, lacy wooden balconies, coloured glazing and roof decorations.

Omani-influenced: a style derived from Omani architecture, characterized by stark geometrical forms and plain walls.

Bibliography

Bandarin, Francesco and Ron van Oers, *The Historic Urban Landscape: Managing Heritage in an Urban Century* (Oxford, Wiley & Sons, 2012).

Baumann, Oscar, *Der Sansibar-Archipel. Ergenbnisse einer mit Unterstützung des Vereins für Erdkunde zu Leipzig 1895/96 ausgeführten Forschungsreise. Zweites Heft. Die Insel Sansibar und ihre kleineren Nachbarinseln* (Leipzig, Duncker & Humblot, 1896).

Bianca, Stefano and Francesco Siravo, *Zanzibar. A plan for the Historic Stone Town* (Geneva, The Aga Khan Trust for Culture, 1996).

Berg, Lawrence D. and Jani Vuolteenaho (eds.), *Critical Toponymies: The Contested Politics of Place Naming* (London, Routledge, 2009).

Bissell, William Cunningham, *Urban Design, Chaos and Colonial Power in Zanzibar* (Indiana, University Press, 2012).

Burton, Richard Francis, *Zanzibar: City, Island and Coast* (London, Tinsley, 1872).

Callenberg, Mia, *Hidden Stories and Urban Values in Zanzibar. History and Heritage-Based Regeneration of Ng'ambo: a pilot study of Mapembeani.* Master's thesis in architecture and urban design (Gothenburg, Chalmers University of Technology, 2015).

Cornelis, Anna, *An Episode of Modernist Planning Abroad. The Case Study of Michenzani, Zanzibar.* Master's thesis MaHS (Leuven, Catholic University of Leuven, 2008).

Department of Urban and Rural Planning et al., *Ng'ambo Local Area Plan* (Zanzibar, 2016).

Fair, Laura, "Kickin' It: Leisure, Politics and Football in Colonial Zanzibar, 1900s-1950s", *Africa: Journal of the International African Institute*, 67, no. 2 (1997), pp. 224-251.

Fair, Laura, *Pastimes and Politics: Culture, Community and Identity in Post-Abolition Urban Zanzibar, 1890-1945* (Ohio, Ohio University Press, 2001).

Fair, Laura, "Remaking Fashion in the Paris of the Indian Ocean: Dress, Performance and Cultural Construction of a Cosmopolitan Zanzibari Identity", in *Fashioning Africa: Power and the Politics of Dress*, ed. Jean Allman (Bloomington, Indiana University Press, 2004).

Fair, Laura, "Voice, Authority, and Memory: The Kiswahili Recordings of Siti binti Saadi", in *Africa Words, African Voices. Critical Practices in Oral History Critical Practices in Oral History*, eds. Luis White, Stephan F. Miescher and David William Cohen (Bloomington, Indiana University Press, 2001).

Fargion, Janet Topp, "The Music of Zenj: Arab-African Crossovers in the Music of Zanzibar", *Journal des Africanistes*, 72 (2002), pp. 203-212.

Fargion, Janet Topp, "The Role of Women in Taarab in Zanzibar: an Historical Examination of a Process of 'Africanisation'", *The World of Music*, 35, no. 2 (1993), pp. 109-125.

Folkers, Antoni, *Modern Architecture in Africa* (Amsterdam, SUN Architecture, 2010).

Folkers, Antoni et al., "Ng'ambo Tuitakayo: Reconnecting the Swahili City", *International Planning History Society Proceedings*, 17, no. 1 (2016), pp. 25-40.

Ghaidan, Usam, *Lamu: A Study in Conservation* (Nairobi, The East African Literature Bureau, 1976).

Guillain, Charles, *Documents sur l'histoire, la géographie et le commerce de l'Afrique orientale*, vols. I-III & collection of prints (Paris, Arthur Bertrand, 1856).

Ingrams, W.H., *Zanzibar: its History and its People* (Abingdon, Frank Cass & Co., 1931).

Kendall, Henry, *The Zanzibar Town Planning Scheme 1958* (Zanzibar, Government of Zanzibar, 1958).

Kequan, Qian, *Zanzibar Town Master Plan 1982* (Zanzibar, Ministry of Lands, Housing, and Construction, 1982).

Lanchester, Henry V., *Zanzibar: A Study in Tropical Town Planning* (Cheltenham, Burrow, 1923).

Longair, Sarah, *Cracks in the Dome: Fractured Histories of Empire in the Zanzibar Museum, 1897-1964* (London, Routledge, 2015).

Lynch, Kevin, *The Image of the City* (Cambridge, Massachusetts, The MIT Press, 1960).

Martin, Stephen H., "Brass Bands and the Beni Phenomenon in Urban East Africa", *African Music*, 7, no. 2 (1991), pp. 72-81.

Meffert, Erich F., *Ajit Singh, Architect, 1910-1986* (Zanzibar, Von-Heute-auf-Morgen Verlag, 2010).

Myers, Garth Andrew, "Colonial Discourse and Africa's Colonized Middle: Ajit Singh's Architecture", *Historical Geography*, 27 (1995), pp. 27-55.

Myers, Garth Andrew, "Naming and Placing the Other: Power and Urban Landscape in Zanzibar", in *Critical Toponymies: The Contested Politics of Place Naming*, eds. Lawrence D. Berg and Jani Vuolteenaho (London, Routledge, 2009).

Myers, Garth Andrew, *Reconstructing Ng'ambo: Town Planning and Development on the 'Other Side' of Zanzibar* (Los Angeles, PhD, University of California, 1993).

Myers, Garth Andrew, "Representing Postcolonial Zanzibar in Contested Literary, Cultural and Political Geographies", in The Postcolonial World, eds. Jyotsna Singh and David D. Kim (London, Routledge, 2016).

Myers, Garth Andrew, "Stupendous Hammer: Colonial and Postcolonial Reconstructions of Zanzibar's 'Other Side'", *Urban Studies*, 32, no. 8 (1993), pp. 1345–1359.

Myers, Garth Andrew, "Sticks and Stones: Colonialism and Zanzibari Housing", *Africa*, 67, no. 2 (1997), pp. 252-272.

Myers, Garth Andrew, *Verandahs of Power: Colonialism and Space in Urban Africa* (Syracuse, Syracuse University Press, 2003).

Nilsson, Sten Åke et al., *Tanzania: Zanzibar: Present Conditions and Future Plans* (Lund, University of Lund, 1969).

Oldenburg, Ray, "Our vanishing third places", *Planning Commissioners Journal*, 25, no. 4 (1997), pp. 6-10.

Pearce, F.B., Zanzibar, *The Island Metropolis of East Africa* (London, T. F. Unwin, 1920).

Rosser, Colin, *Urbanization in Tropical Africa: a Demographic Introduction* (New York, International Urbanization Survey of the Ford Foundation, 1973).

Shapira Hellerman Planners, *Structure Plan and Urban Development Policy for Zanzibar Town* (Zanzibar, Revolutionary Government of Zanzibar, President's Office Finance, Economy and Development Planning, 2015).

Sheriff, Abdul (ed.), *The History and Conservation of Zanzibar Stone Town* (Ohio, Ohio University Press, 1995).

Scholz, Hubert, *Zanzibar Town Planning Scheme 1968* (Zanzibar, Revolutionary Government of Zanzibar, 1968).

UNESCO, *Recommendation on the Historic Urban Landscape*. Adopted by the General Conference at its 36th session, 10 November 2011, Paris.

van Oers, Ron (ed.), *Swahili Historic Urban Landscapes: Report on the Historic Urban Landscape Workshops and Field Activities on the Swahili Coast in East Africa 2011-2012* (Paris, France, UNESCO World Heritage Centre, 2013).

Wimmelbücker, Ludger, "Architecture and City Planning Projects of the German Democratic Republic in Zanzibar", *The Journal of Architecture*, 17, no. 3, 2012 pp. 407-432.

Zanzibar Tourist Information Bureau, *A Guide to Zanzibar* (London, The Crown Agencies for the Colonies, 1961).

Related Reading:

Bakari, Mohammed Ali, *The Democratisation Process in Zanzibar: A Retarded Transition* (Hamburg, Insitut für Afrika-Kunde, 2001).

Chauvin, Amélie and Alexandra Papadaki, *'The Other Side', an Architectural Insight for the Urban Metamorphosis of an East-African City: the Case of Zanzibar Town*, MA thesis (Gothenburg, Chalmers University of Technology, 2014).

Department of Urban and Rural Planning, *Enabling Transformation of Zanzibar: National Spatial Development Strategy* (Zanzibar, 2014).

Aga Khan Trust for Culture, *Conservation and Design Guidelines for Zanzibar Stone Town* (Geneva, Aga Khan Trust for Culture, 1994).

Fair, Laura, "Hollywood Hegemony? Hardly: Audience Preferences in Zanzibar, 1950s-1970s", *Zanzibar International Film Festival Journal*, 1, no. 1 (2004), pp. 52-58.

Fargion, Janet Topp, *Taarab Music in Zanzibar in the Twentieth Century: A Story of 'Old is Gold' and Flying Spirits* (London, Routledge, 2014).

Folkers, Antoni, "Planning and Re-planning Ng'ambo, Zanzibar", *South African Journal on Architectural History* (SAJAH), 29, no. 1 (2014), pp. 39-53.

Folkers, Antoni (ed.), *Mtoni: Palace, Sultan & Princess of Zanzibar* (Utrecht, ArchiAfrika, 2010).

Freeman-Grenville, G. S. P., *The Swahili Coast, 2nd to 19th Centuries: Islam, Christianity and Commerce in Eastern Africa* (London, Variorum, 1988).

Ghaidan, Usam, *Lamu: A Study of the Swahili Town* (Nairobi, The East African Literature Bureau, 1975).

Garlake, Peter, *Early Art and Architecture of Africa* (Oxford, Oxford University Press, 2002).

Garlake, Peter, *Early Islamic Architecture of the East African Coast* (Oxford, Oxford University Press, 1966).

Juma, Abdurahman, *The Omani Affinities of the Nineteenth-Century Houses on the East African Coast: An Archaeological Study* (Paper, University of Cambridge, 1987).

Juma, Abdurahman, *Unguja Ukuu on Zanzibar: An Archaeological Study of Early Urbanism. Vol. 3 of Studies in Global Archaeology* (Uppsala, Uppsala University, 2004).

Kirkman, J., *Men and Monuments of the East African Coast* (London, Lutterworth, 1964).

Menon, Robert, *Zanzibar in the Nineteenth Century: Aspects of Urban Development in an East African Costal Town*, MA thesis (Los Angeles, University of California, 1978).

Middleton, John, *The World of the Swahili: African Mercantile Civilization* (New Haven, Connecticut, Yale University Press, 1992).

Myers, Garth Andrew and Harris, R., "Hybrid Housing Improvement and Control in Late Colonial Zanzibar", *Journal of the Society of Architectural Historians*, 66, no. 4 (2007), pp. 476-493.

Myers, Garth Andrew, "Making the Socialist City of Zanzibar", *Geographical Review*, 84, no.4 (1993), pp. 451-464.

Myers, Garth Andrew, "Intellectual of Empire: Eric Dutton and Hegemony in British Africa", *Annals of the Association of American Geographers*, 88, no.1 (1998), pp. 1-27.

Myers, Garth Andrew, "Social Construction of Peri-Urban Places and Alternative Planning in Zanzibar", *African Affairs*, 109, no. 437 (2010), pp. 575–595.

Petterson, Don, *Revolution in Zanzibar: An American's Cold War Tale* (Boulder, Colorado, Westview Press, 2002).

Reinwald, Brigitte, "Tonight at the Empire: Cinema and Urbanity in Zanzibar, 1920s to 1960", *Afrique & Histoire*, 5, no. 1 (2006), pp. 81-109.

Sheriff, Abdul, *Slaves, Spices & Ivory in Zanzibar: Integration of an East African Commercial Empire into the World Economy, 1770–1873* (Ohio, Ohio University Press, 1987).

Sheriff, Abdul, *Dhow Cultures of the Indian Ocean: Cosmopolitan, Commerce and Islam* (London, C. Hurst & Co, 2010).

Siravo, Francesco and Ann Pulver, *Planning Lamu: Conservation of an East African Sea Port* (Nairobi, National Museums of Kenya, 1986).

Sollien, Silje, *Transforming the Other Side of Ilha de Moçambique*. PhD Thesis (Copenhagen, Royal Institute for the Arts, 2014).

Strandes, Justus, *The Portuguese Period in East Africa* (Nairobi, East African Literature Bureau, 1971).

Sutton, J. E. G. (ed.), *Archaeological Sites of East Africa: Four Studies, Azania*, Special Volume XXXIII (Nairobi, The British Institute in Eastern Africa, 1998).

UNESCO, *World Heritage and Buffer Zones* (Paris, World Heritage Centre, 2009).

UNESCO, *Policy for the Integration of a Sustainable Development Perspective into the Processes of the World Heritage Convention*, Resolution 20 GA 13, 20th Session (Paris, 2015).

Illustration Credits

The authors have made all reasonable efforts to trace the rights holders to any copyrighted material used in this work. In cases where these efforts have not been successful, the publisher welcomes communications from copyright holders so that the appropriate acknowledgements can be made in future editions, and further permission matters settled.

Map credits:

Historical Maps and Plans
All maps copyright Department of Urban and Rural Planning Zanzibar, unless otherwise stated.

Map V: Map of Zanzibar Town by Oscar Baumann (1895). Source: Public Domain.
Map VI: Zanzibar Town Improvement Scheme by H.V. Lanchester (1923). Source: *Zanzibar: A Study in Tropical Town Planning* (Cheltenham, Burrow, 1923).
Map XI: *Zanzibar Town Planning Scheme: Proposed Land Use by H. Scholz (1968).* Courtesy of H. Scholz.
Map XV: *Borders of the World Heritage Site, Stone Town (1999).* Source: UNESCO, WHS Stone Town of Zanzibar, Map A, showing the extent of the conservation area.

Survey Maps

Maps XIX-XXXII Copyright African Architecture Matters

Figure credits:

Introduction Image:

African Architecture Matters

Chapter 1:

1.0 Mieke Woestenburg
1.1 Department of Urban and Rural Planning Zanzibar/ African Architecture Matters
1.2 Zanzibar National Archives
1.3-1.4 Chinouk Jongerius, Tinka Jongerius and Renske de Meijer
1.5 Sketch by Antoni Folkers. Redrawn with permission from Ohio University Press.
Drawing after Laura Fair in *Pastimes & Politics. culture, community, and Identity in Post-abolition Urban Zanzibar, 1890-1945* (Ohio, Ohio University Press, 2001), p. 119.
1.6 Department of Urban and Rural Planning Zanzibar/ African Architecture Matters
1.7 Courtesy of Antoni Folkers
1.8-1.9 Zanzibar National Archives
1.10 Berend van der Lans/ African Architecture Matters
1.11 Courtesy of Antoni Folkers
1.12 Chinouk Jongerius, Tinka Jongerius and Renske de Meijer
1.13 Source: H. V. Lanchester, Zanzibar: A Study in Tropical Town Planning (Cheltenham, Burrow, 1923).
1.14 Courtesy of Livia Wang, image reprinted with permission from Longair, Sarah. *Cracks in the Dome: Fractures Histories of Empire in the Zanzibar Museum, 1897-1964* (London, Routledge, 2015).
1.15 Department of Urban and Rural Planning Zanzibar/ African Architecture Matters
1.16 Department of Urban and Rural Planning Zanzibar
1.17 Zanzibar National Archives
1.18 Sketch by Antoni Folkers. Redrawn with permission from Ohio University Press. Drawing after Laura Fair in *Pastimes & Politics. culture, community, and Identity in Post-abolition Urban Zanzibar, 1890-1945* (Ohio, Ohio University Press, 2001), p. 138.
1.19 Department of Urban and Rural Planning Zanzibar
1.20 Zanzibar National Archives
1.21-1.22 Department of Urban and Rural Planning Zanzibar
1.23 Zanzibar National Archives
1.24 African Architecture Matters
1.25-1.26 Sketch by Belinda van Buiten
1.27 Source: H. V. Lanchester, *Zanzibar: A Study in Tropical Town Planning* (Cheltenham, Burrow, 1923).
1.28 Zanzibar National Archives
1.29 Mia Callenberg
1.30 Department of Urban and Rural Planning Zanzibar
1.31 Department of Urban and Rural Planning Zanzibar
1.32 Zanzibar National Archives
1.33-1.34 Sketch by Antoni Folkers
1.35 Sketch by Belinda van Buiten
1.36 Courtesy of Capital Art Studio
1.37 Sketch by Antoni Folkers
1.38 Amélie Chauvin/ African Architecture Matters
1.39 Courtesy of Sten Åke Nilsson
1.40 Courtesy of Capital Art Studio
1.41 Mieke Woestenburg
1.42 Zanzibar National Archives
1.43 Mieke Woestenburg
1.44 Courtesy of Antoni Folkers
1.45 Department of Urban and Rural Planning Zanzibar
1.46 Zanzibar National Archives
1.47 Courtesy of Capital Art Studio
1.48 Anna Cornelis
1.49-1.50 Courtesy of Sten Åke Nilsson
1.51 Courtesy of Capital Art Studio
1.52 Courtesy family of K.H. Nøstvik
1.53-1.54 Department of Urban and Rural Planning Zanzibar
1.55 Department of Urban and Rural Planning Zanzibar/ African Architecture Matters
1.56 Alexandra Papadaki
1.57 Copyright Aga Khan Trust for Culture / R. Marks
1.58-1.60 Department of Urban and Rural Planning Zanzibar

1.61 Sketches by Antoni Folkers
1.62 Chalmers University
1.63-1.64 Department of Urban and Rural Planning Zanzibar/ African Architecture Matters
1.65 Mia Callenberg/ Chalmers University
1.66 African Architecture Matters

Chapter 2:

2.0 Rahim Saggaf Photography
2.1 Sketch by Antoni Folkers (left) and African Architecture Matters (right)
2.2 Sketches by Amélie Chauvin
2.3 -2.4 Department of Urban and Rural Planning Zanzibar/ African Architecture Matters
2.5 Alexandra Papadaki/ African Architecture Matters
2.6-2.22 Department of Urban and Rural Planning Zanzibar/ African Architecture Matters
2.23-2.25 Marie Morel/ African Architecture Matters
2.26-2.27 Zanzibar National Archives
2.28 Rahim Saggaf Photography
2.29 African Architecture Matters
2.30 Iga Perzyna/ African Architecture Matters
2.31-2.32 Courtesy of Capital Art Studio
2.33 Berend van der Lans / African Architecture Matters
2.34-2.36 Sketch by Belinda van Buiten
2.37-2.44 Department of Urban and Rural Planning Zanzibar/ African Architecture Matters
2.45 Zanzibar National Archives
2.46 Iga Perzyna/ African Architecture Matters
2.47 Zanzibar National Archives
2.48-2.49 Courtesy of Capital Art Studio
2.50 African Architecture Matters
2.51 Chinouk Jongerius, Tinka Jongerius and Renske de Meijer
2.52 Department of Urban and Rural Planning Zanzibar/ African Architecture Matters
2.53 Mia Callenberg
2.54 Department of Urban and Rural Planning Zanzibar/ African Architecture Matters
2.55 Mia Callenberg
2.56-2.59 Department of Urban and Rural Planning Zanzibar/ African Architecture Matters
2.60 Mieke Woestenburg
2.61-2.62 Department of Urban and Rural Planning Zanzibar/ African Architecture Matters
2.63-2.64 Zanzibar National Archives
2.65 Department of Urban and Rural Planning Zanzibar/ African Architecture Matters
2.66 Rahim Saggaf Photography
2.67 Department of Urban and Rural Planning Zanzibar/ African Architecture Matters
2.68 Paulina i Michał Mikołajczak. Source: www.addicted2travel.pl.
2.69-2.72 Department of Urban and Rural Planning Zanzibar/ African Architecture Matters
2.73 Christoph Montebelli
2.74-2.77 Department of Urban and Rural Planning Zanzibar/ African Architecture Matters
2.78-2.79 Zanzibar National Archives
2.80 Rahim Saggaf Photography
2.81-2.82 Department of Urban and Rural Planning Zanzibar/ African Architecture Matters
2.83 Zanzibar National Archives
2.84 Courtesy of Abdulghani Msoma
2.85-2.88 Department of Urban and Rural Planning Zanzibar/ African Architecture Matters

Chapter 3:

3.0 Amélie Chauvin/ African Architecture Matters
3.1 Christoph Montebelli
3.2-3.3 Amélie Chauvin/ African Architecture Matters
3.4 African Architecture Matters

Chapter 4:

4.0 Mieke Woestenburg
4.1-4.6 African Architecture Matters
4.7 Alexandra Papadaki
4.8 African Architecture Matters

Chapter 5:

5.0 African Architecture Matters
5.1-5.5 Department of Urban and Rural Planning Zanzibar/ African Architecture Matters

This atlas was produced by the Department of Urban and Rural Planning, Zanzibar and African Architecture Matters

Text: Antoni Folkers, Iga Perzyna, Marie Morel and Muhammad Juma Muhammad

Peer reviewers: Nicole Bolomey, Berend van der Lans, Mwalim A. Mwalim, Aart Oxenaar, Abdul Sheriff, Farouk Topan

Editors: Antoni Folkers and Iga Perzyna

Copy editing and proofreading: Rodney Bolt

Graphic design: Amélie Chauvin

Maps: Alexandra Papadaki

Distribution: LM Publishers, the Netherlands
African Studies Centre Leiden, the Netherlands

www.lmpublishers.nl
info@lmpublishers.nl

ISBN: 978-94-6022-517-8

This publication has been made possible through the generous financial support from:

Ministry of Foreign Affairs

creative industries fund NL

Netherlands Enterprise Agency

City of Amsterdam

EFL STICHTING